Jessica Smith

Criminal Proceedings before North Carolina Magistrates

2014

The School of Government at the University of North Carolina at Chapel Hill works to improve the lives of North Carolinians by engaging in practical scholarship that helps public officials and citizens understand and improve state and local government. Established in 1931 as the Institute of Government, the School provides educational, advisory, and research services for state and local governments. The School of Government is also home to a nationally ranked graduate program in public administration and specialized centers focused on information technology and environmental finance.

As the largest university-based local government training, advisory, and research organization in the United States, the School of Government offers up to 200 courses, webinars, and specialized conferences for more than 12,000 public officials each year. In addition, faculty members annually publish approximately 50 books, manuals, reports, articles, bulletins, and other print and online content related to state and local government. Each day that the General Assembly is in session, the School produces the *Daily Bulletin Online*, which reports on the day's activities for members of the legislature and others who need to follow the course of legislation.

The Master of Public Administration Program is offered in two formats. The full-time, two-year residential program serves up to 60 students annually. In 2013 the School launched MPA@UNC, an online format designed for working professionals and others seeking flexibility while advancing their careers in public service. The School's MPA program consistently ranks among the best public administration graduate programs in the country, particularly in city management. With courses ranging from public policy analysis to ethics and management, the program educates leaders for local, state, and federal governments and nonprofit organizations.

Operating support for the School of Government's programs and activities comes from many sources, including state appropriations, local government membership dues, private contributions, publication sales, course fees, and service contracts. Visit www.sog.unc.edu or call 919.966.5381 for more information on the School's courses, publications, programs, and services.

Michael R. Smith, Dean
Thomas H. Thornburg, Senior Associate Dean
Frayda S. Bluestein, Associate Dean for Faculty Development
L. Ellen Bradley, Associate Dean for Programs and Marketing
Johnny Burleson, Associate Dean for Development
Todd A. Nicolet, Associate Dean for Operations
Bradley G. Volk, Associate Dean for Administration

FACULTY

Whitney Afonso
Trey Allen
Gregory S. Allison
David N. Ammons
Ann M. Anderson
Maureen Berner
Mark F. Botts
Michael Crowell
Leisha DeHart-Davis
Shea Riggsbee Denning
Sara DePasquale
James C. Drennan
Richard D. Ducker
Joseph S. Ferrell
Alyson A. Grine
Norma Houston
Cheryl Daniels Howell
Jeffrey A. Hughes
Willow S. Jacobson
Robert P. Joyce
Diane M. Juffras
Dona G. Lewandowski
Adam Lovelady

James M. Markham
Christopher B. McLaughlin
Kara A. Millonzi
Jill D. Moore
Jonathan Q. Morgan
Ricardo S. Morse
C. Tyler Mulligan
Kimberly L. Nelson
David W. Owens
LaToya B. Powell
William C. Rivenbark
Dale J. Roenigk
John Rubin
Jessica Smith
Meredith Smith
Carl W. Stenberg III
John B. Stephens
Charles Szypszak
Shannon H. Tufts
Vaughn Mamlin Upshaw
Aimee N. Wall
Jeffrey B. Welty
Richard B. Whisnant

Contents

Preface

This publication replaces my "Criminal Procedure for Magistrates," *Administration of Justice Bulletin* No. 2009/08 (Dec. 2009), and serves as the new criminal procedure text for the School of Government's Basic School for Magistrates. It summarizes criminal procedure for North Carolina magistrates and is current through the 2013 legislative session and appellate cases through December 31, 2013.

Coverage includes criminal process and pleadings, initial appearance, pretrial release, fugitives, and search warrants. This publication does not address a magistrate's authority under Section 7A-273 of the North Carolina General Statutes to accept guilty pleas or admissions of responsibility for infractions and certain Class 3 misdemeanors, commonly called waiver list jurisdiction. Listings of the offenses subject to waiver list jurisdiction are available online at www.nccourts.org/Courts/Trial/Costs/CurrentW.asp.

Jessica Smith
Summer 2014

I. Criminal Process and Pleadings

Magistrates issue and encounter five different types of criminal process and pleadings in their daily work. They are the

1. citation,
2. criminal summons,
3. warrant for arrest,
4. order for arrest (OFA), and
5. magistrate's order.

Other types of pleadings, including the statement of charges, information, and indictment, are not part of a magistrate's daily work and thus are not discussed in this publication.

The purpose of criminal process is to require a person to come to court.[1] When a warrant for arrest or OFA is issued, this is accomplished by taking the person into custody and setting conditions of release designed to, among other things, ensure the defendant's appearance in court. When a citation or criminal summons is used, it is accomplished by ordering the person to appear in court.

Most forms of criminal process can also serve as the criminal pleading; the OFA is the only type of criminal process that cannot serve as a pleading.[2] Criminal pleadings have three main functions: to give the court jurisdiction to enter judgment on the offense charged, to give the defendant notice of the charges, and to allow the defendant to raise a double jeopardy defense.[3] In order to serve all three functions, the documents must be issued properly. The sections that follow will help magistrates do that. Table 1 provides a quick reference on the five forms of process and pleadings encountered by magistrates.

A. Types of Process and Pleadings

1. Citation

Statute: G.S. 15A-302

Key N.C. Administrative Office of the Courts (AOC) forms:

   AOC-CR-500 (uniform citation),

   AOC-CR-501 (uniform citation; for assignment by State Highway Patrol),

---

1. Official Commentary to Article 17 of the North Carolina General Statutes (hereinafter G.S.), Chapter 15A.

2. G.S. 15A-921, -922.

3. State v. Greer, 238 N.C. 325, 328 (1953).

>   AOC-CR-502/ALE/ABC (uniform citation; for assignment by Alcohol Law Enforcement and
>   Alcoholic Beverage Control),
>   AOC-CR-503/Wildlife/Forestry (uniform citation; for assignment by Wildlife and Forestry
>   Resources),
>   AOC-CR-504 (uniform citation; for assignment by Norfolk Southern Railway).

Many officers now issue citations through eCITATION, a system that automates the transfer of citation data directly from a law enforcement officer's patrol car to the courts and does not require the use of paper forms. However, most officers use eCITATION only in cases where the defendant is not arrested and thus does not need to be taken before a magistrate. In addition, as of this writing, the eCITATION system has not been linked to the North Carolina Statewide Warrant Repository (NCAWARE). For these reasons, magistrates are unlikely to see citations created in eCITATION in their daily work.

a. Defined. A citation is a directive that a person appear in court to answer a charge.[4]

b. Who may issue. A citation is issued by a law enforcement officer or other person authorized by statute who has probable cause to believe that a person has committed a misdemeanor or infraction.[5] Magistrates do not have statutory authority to issue citations. As noted, a citation may be issued by a law enforcement officer "or other person authorized by statute." An example of a statute that authorizes persons other than law enforcement officers to issue citations is the littering statute, G.S. 14-399. That law provides that for the purposes of that section, "any employee of a county or municipality designated by the county or municipality as a litter enforcement officer" may enforce the statute.[6]

c. Used for misdemeanors and infractions. A citation may be used for any misdemeanor or infraction, though it is used most often for traffic cases.[7] Legally, the citation is not limited to on-the-scene situations, and it may be issued any time a citizen provides a law enforcement officer with probable cause to believe that a defendant committed a misdemeanor or infraction. For example, an officer could use a citation to charge a person with shoplifting instead of arresting the person.

d. Contents. Although officers issue citations, magistrates sometimes opt to convert a citation to a magistrate's order rather than complete an entirely new magistrate's order. See section I.A.4.d, below (describing this procedure). Once the conversion is accomplished, the citation becomes an order of the magistrate. Thus, before converting a citation, the magistrate should carefully check its form.

The citation must

- identify the crime charged, including the date, and where material, the property and other persons involved;
- list the name and address of the person cited or provide other identification if that cannot be determined;
- identify the officer issuing the citation; and
- direct the person to whom the citation is issued to appear in a designated court at a designated time and date.[8]

---

4. G.S. 15A-302(a); Sykes v. Hiatt, 98 N.C. App. 688, 691 (1990).

5. G.S. 15A-302(a), (b); State v. Hamilton, 125 N.C. App. 396, 400 (1997).

6. G.S. 14-399(i)(3) & (j).

7. G.S. 15A-302(b).

8. G.S. 15A-302(c); State v. Phillips, 149 N.C. App. 310, 316 (2002) (citation satisfied the statutory requirements).

Table 1. Forms of Process and Pleadings Encountered by Magistrates

	Citation	Summons	Warrant for Arrest	Magistrate's Order	Order for Arrest
Who Issues?	Officer or other authorized person	Judicial official[a]	Judicial official[a]	Judicial official[a]	Judicial official[a]
What Can It Charge?	Misdemeanor or infraction	Any crime or infraction[b]	Any crime	Any crime	N/A
What Does It Do?	Directs a person to appear in court	Directs a person to appear in court	Orders an officer to arrest person	Finds an officer's warrantless arrest was proper	Orders an officer to arrest person

a. A judicial official includes a magistrate, clerk, judge, or justice of the General Court of Justice. G.S. 15A-101(5).
b. Because of the way it is drafted, the AOC Criminal Summons form cannot be used for felonies.

The citation is effective even if a defendant refuses to sign it.[9] In this situation, the officer may write "defendant refused to sign" in the space for the defendant's signature.

If there are two charges, the officer should use the lower portion of the citation to write out the second charge; two offenses should not be charged on the top half of the form. If there are more than two charges, the officer should use a separate citation for every two charges. These procedures are required because each charge against a defendant must be pleaded in a separate count,[10] and the AOC uniform citation form is drafted for only two counts per form.

e. Failure to appear (FTA). Because a citation is not issued by a judicial official, a defendant who fails to appear in court cannot be charged with criminal contempt under G.S. 5A-11(a)(3). If the defendant fails to appear in court on a citation for a misdemeanor, an OFA may be issued.[11] If the defendant fails to appear in court on a citation for an infraction, a criminal summons may be issued.[12] An arrest warrant cannot be used for a FTA on an infraction.[13] If the defendant fails to appear in court when charged with an infraction in a criminal summons, the presiding judge may issue an order to show cause for contempt (but not an OFA, unless it is issued with the order to show cause under G.S. 5A-16(b)).

f. Issuing a summons or warrant after a citation has been issued. The fact that a citation has been issued for a misdemeanor does not prevent the later issuance of a summons or warrant for that offense.[14] For example, suppose an officer cites a defendant for a misdemeanor and later wants to arrest that defendant. The citation cannot be used to take the defendant into custody. An arrest warrant is needed if the defendant is not already in the officer's custody and the officer has no basis for a warrantless arrest. If the officer appears before a magistrate for an arrest warrant, the officer

---

9. G.S. 15A-302(d).
10. G.S. 15A-924(a)(2); State v. Rogers, 68 N.C. App. 358, 378 (1984); State v. Beaver, 14 N.C. App. 459, 461 (1972).
11. G.S. 15A-302(f); -305(b)(3).
12. G.S. 15A-1116(b).
13. *Id.*
14. G.S. 15A-302(f).

must swear to the facts and the magistrate should follow the procedures set forth below for issuing an arrest warrant. If the officer has issued a citation and has the defendant in custody, the proper process is a magistrate's order, discussed in section I.A.4.a, below.

2. Criminal Summons

Statute: G.S. 15A-303

Key AOC forms:

 AOC-CR-113 (misdemeanor criminal summons),

 AOC-CR-115 (misdemeanor worthless check).

a. Defined. A criminal summons consists of a statement of the crime or infraction charged and an order directing the accused to appear in court and answer the charges; it does not order a law enforcement officer to take the defendant into custody.[15] A criminal summons is based on a showing of probable cause supported by oath or affirmation.[16]

b. Who may issue. A criminal summons is issued by a justice, judge, clerk, or magistrate.[17]

c. Used for any crime or infraction. A criminal summons legally may be used for any felony, misdemeanor, or infraction.[18] However, the AOC criminal summons form is not drafted to charge a felony and should not be used for that purpose.

d. Contents. A criminal summons must contain a statement of the crime or infraction charged.[19] Using the appropriate charging language (see section I.B.4, below) and following the guidelines for criminal pleadings (see section I.B.9, below) will ensure that the summons contains a proper statement.

The summons must order the defendant to appear in a designated court at a designated time and date to answer the charges.[20] Typically the date set is the officer's next court date. Except for cause noted in the criminal summons by the issuing official, an appearance date may not be set more than one month following the date the summons is issued.[21] The summons must advise the defendant that he or she may be held in contempt of court for failure to appear as directed.[22]

e. Warrant for arrest may issue after summons has issued. If the offense charged is a crime, the issuance of a criminal summons does not bar the later issuance of a warrant for arrest.[23]

f. Failure to appear. A defendant who fails to appear as ordered in a criminal summons may be held in contempt of court.[24] In addition, if the offense charged is a crime (misdemeanor or felony), the presiding judge may issue an OFA.[25]

---

15. G.S. 15A-303(a).
16. *Id.*
17. G.S. 15A-303(f), -304(f).
18. G.S. 15A-303(a).
19. G.S. 15A-303(b).
20. G.S. 15A-303(d).
21. *Id.*
22. *Id.*
23. G.S. 15A-303(e)(1).
24. G.S. 15A-303(e)(3).
25. G.S. 15A-303(e)(2).

3. Warrant for Arrest

Statute: G.S. 15A-304

Key AOC forms:

AOC-CR-100 (warrant for arrest),

AOC-CR-107 (warrant for arrest–misdemeanor, worthless checks).

a. Defined. A warrant for arrest consists of a statement of the crime charged and an order directing that the accused be arrested and held to answer the charges.[26] Thus, unlike the citation and criminal summons, which merely direct an individual to appear in court to answer charges, the warrant for arrest directs law enforcement officers to arrest the accused. The warrant must be based on a showing of probable cause that the defendant committed a crime.[27] That showing may be made on oath or affirmation.[28]

b. Who may issue. A warrant for arrest may be issued by a justice, judge, clerk, or magistrate.[29]

c. Used for any crime. A warrant for arrest may be used for any crime, whether a misdemeanor or felony.[30] It may not be used for an infraction.[31]

d. Contents. A warrant for arrest must contain a statement of the crime charged.[32] Using the appropriate charging language (see section I.B.4, below) and following the guidelines for criminal pleadings (see section I.B.9, below), will ensure that the warrant contains a proper statement. The warrant must direct a law enforcement officer to take the defendant into custody and to bring the defendant, without unnecessary delay, before a judicial official.[33]

e. When issued: Warrant versus summons. G.S. 15A-304(b) provides that a warrant may be used instead of or after a summons has been issued when the person needs to be taken into custody. If the person already has been taken into custody under a warrantless arrest, the proper procedure is to complete a magistrate's order, not a warrant, as discussed in section I.A.4.a, below.

G.S. 15A-304(b) directs that the circumstances to be considered in determining whether the person should be taken into custody may include, but are not limited to, the following:

- failure to appear when previously summoned,
- facts making it apparent that a person summoned will fail to appear,
- danger that the accused will escape,
- danger that there may be injury to a person or property, and
- seriousness of the offense.

Note that under G.S. 15A-502 a person charged with a misdemeanor or felony may be fingerprinted upon arrest, if allowed by the local fingerprint plan adopted pursuant to G.S. 15A-1383. Issuance of a warrant will lead to an arrest; issuance of a summons will not.

---

26. G.S. 15A-304(a).

27. *Id.*; State v. Sturdivant, 304 N.C. 293, 298 (1981).

28. G.S. 15A-304(a); State v. Bullin, 150 N.C. App. 631, 638 (2002).

29. G.S. 15A-304(f).

30. G.S. 15A-304.

31. *Id.* (authorizing issuance only for a "crime").

32. G.S. 15A-304(c).

33. G.S. 15A-304(e).

Magistrates should follow the local policy issued by the senior resident superior court judge or chief district court judge on whether a summons or warrant is appropriate. In the absence of a specific policy, many magistrates apply the following guidelines:

- For infractions, a summons is used.
- For felonies, a warrant is used.
- For misdemeanors, a summons should be used
  - when the person is likely to appear in court without conditions of pretrial release and
  - for most minor misdemeanors, unless there is a flight risk.

f. Cross warrants. G.S. 15A-304(d) provides that a judicial official may not refuse to issue a warrant solely because a prior warrant has been issued for the arrest of another person involved in the same matter. A judicial official retains discretion to issue a criminal summons instead of an arrest warrant in such instances.

g. Arrest warrant for a fugitive. AOC-CR-910M is the form for an arrest warrant for a fugitive. It has a different purpose from that of the warrant for arrest discussed in this section. The arrest warrant for a fugitive is discussed in section IV, below.

4. Magistrate's Order

Statute: G.S. 15A-511(c)

Key AOC form:

AOC-CR-116 (magistrate's order).

a. When used. A magistrate's order is used only when a defendant has been arrested without a warrant.[34] When a defendant is arrested without a warrant, he or she must be brought, without unnecessary delay, to a magistrate for an initial appearance.[35] If the magistrate finds that there is probable cause to charge the defendant with a crime, the magistrate must issue a magistrate's order.

b. Used for any crime. The magistrate's order may be used for any crime, both felonies and misdemeanors.[36]

c. Contents. A magistrate's order must contain a statement of the crime, as required for a warrant for arrest, and a finding that the defendant has been arrested without a warrant and there is probable cause for detention.[37]

d. Conversion of citation. Sometimes an officer will issue a citation and then arrest the defendant and bring him or her before a magistrate. Instead of creating a new magistrate's order, the officer's citation may be converted into a magistrate's order. This can be done by checking the block on the citation titled "Magistrate's Order—Misdemeanor Only." In NCAWARE the conversion is accomplished by entering the citation information into the system as a magistrate's order based on a general citation. The relevant information can be pre-entered by an officer. But of course, the officer cannot issue the magistrate's order; only a judicial official can do that.

e. Magistrate's order for fugitive. AOC-CR-909M is the form for a magistrate's order for a fugitive. It has a different purpose from that of the magistrate's order discussed in this section. The magistrate's order for a fugitive form is discussed in section IV, below.

---

34. G.S. 15A-511(c).
35. See section II.B.1, below.
36. G.S. 15A-511(c).
37. G.S. 15A-511(c)(3).

5. Order for Arrest

Statute: G.S. 15A-305

Key AOC form:

AOC-CR-217 (order for arrest).

a. Defined. An OFA is an order that a law enforcement officer take a person into custody.[38]

b. Who may issue. An OFA may be issued by a justice, judge, clerk, or magistrate.[39]

c. When issued. G.S. 15A-305(b) lists all of the circumstances in which an OFA may be issued. For example, an OFA may be issued when a defendant fails to appear after being released on conditions of pretrial release or fails to appear as directed in a criminal summons. However, a magistrate is likely to issue an OFA in only one circumstance: when a defendant is released subject to conditions, violates those conditions, and needs to be brought back before the magistrate—but only if this happens *before* the first appearance in district court.[40] The reason for this rule is that once the case has proceeded to district court, jurisdiction lies in the trial court division and the magistrate is divested of jurisdiction to act.

d. Contents. When a magistrate issues an OFA, the order must state why it is being issued and direct an officer to take the defendant into custody and bring the defendant before the court.[41]

B. Procedure for Issuing Process and Pleadings

Before issuing criminal process and pleadings, a magistrate must determine

- that probable cause exists,
- which crime(s) to charge,
- what charging language to use, and
- which type of process or pleading to issue.

This publication focuses on all but the second of these inquiries. New magistrates will learn more about which crime(s) to charge in sessions on the elements of crimes during Basic School for Magistrates. The School of Government publication JESSICA SMITH, NORTH CAROLINA CRIMES: A GUIDEBOOK ON THE ELEMENTS OF CRIME (UNC School of Government, 7th ed. 2012) (hereinafter NORTH CAROLINA CRIMES), describes the more commonly charged North Carolina crimes. Note that NORTH CAROLINA CRIMES is updated annually with a cumulative supplement. Hard copies of the book are purchased and provided to each magistrate by the North Carolina Administrative Office of the Courts.[42]

---

38. G.S. 15A-305(a).

39. G.S. 15A-305(a) & (d).

40. G.S. 15A-305(b)(5); -534(e).

41. G.S. 15A-305(c).

42. An online version of the CRIMES book is available for an annual subscription charge; information can be found at www.sog.unc.edu/node/2243.

1. Independent Determination

Magistrates are independent judicial officials, not agents of law enforcement.[43] Thus, when a magistrate determines whether to issue criminal process and pleadings, the determination must be neutral and independent.[44]

2. Restrictions on Issuing Process

The general assembly has limited a magistrate's ability to issue criminal process in certain situations. These situations are discussed below.

a. Certain defendants who are school employees. G.S. 15A-301(b1) provides that a magistrate may not issue criminal process against a school employee (defined in G.S. 14-33(c)(6)) for an offense that occurred while the school employee was discharging his or her duties of employment without the prior written approval of the district attorney or the district attorney's designee. This subsection does not apply if the offense

- is a traffic offense or
- occurred in the presence of a sworn law enforcement officer.[45]

The district attorney may decline to accept the authority to pre-approve criminal process under the statute by sending a letter to the chief district court judge.[46] The chief district court judge then must appoint a magistrate to review applications for criminal process against school employees that allege misdemeanor offenses committed in the discharge of the duties of employment.[47] The statute does not address what happens to felony charges if the district attorney declines authority to approve criminal process. And the requirements do not apply when there is no appointed magistrate available to review the application.[48] In addition, failure to comply with the statute's requirements does not affect the validity of the criminal process.[49]

b. Obscenity offenses. G.S. 14-190.20 provides that a search warrant or criminal process for obscenity offenses in violation of G.S. 14-190.1 through -190.5 may be issued only upon the request of a prosecutor.[50]

---

43. United States v. Leon, 468 U.S. 897, 914 (1984) ("the courts must . . . insist that the magistrate purport to perform his neutral and detached function and not serve merely as a rubber stamp for the police") (quotation omitted).

44. Giordenello v. United States, 357 U.S. 480, 486 (1958) ("The purpose of the complaint . . . is to enable the appropriate magistrate . . . to determine whether the 'probable cause' required to support a warrant exists. The [magistrate] must judge for himself the persuasiveness of the facts relied on by a complaining officer to show probable cause. He should not accept without question the complainant's mere conclusion that the person whose arrest is sought has committed a crime."); State v. Matthews, 270 N.C. 35, 40–41 (1967) (relying on *Giordenello* to hold that a "desk officer" appointed by the chief of police was not a "neutral and detached magistrate" and therefore that the desk officer's order for arrest was "invalid for failure to meet the requirements of the Fourth and Fourteenth Amendments to the Constitution of the United States"); *see also* G.S. 15A-304(d) (judicial official must make an "independent judgment that there is probable cause").

45. G.S. 15A-301(b1).

46. G.S. 15A-301(b1) & (b2).

47. G.S. 15A-301(b2).

48. *Id.*

49. *Id.*

50. *See* Cinema I Video, Inc. v. Thornburg, 83 N.C. App. 544, 564 (1986) *aff'd*, 320 N.C. 485 (1987) (noting this provision).

c. Habitual felon and related statuses. The habitual felon statute provides that the decision of whether to charge a defendant as a habitual felon is to be made by the "district attorney, in his or her discretion."[51] The habitual breaking and entering statute contains similar language.[52] The violent habitual felon statute does not speak to this issue, but given the close connection between the habitual offender statutes, it is probably best to leave to the district attorney the decision of whether to charge a defendant as a violent habitual felon. Thus, magistrates should not charge a defendant with being a habitual felon, a violent habitual felon, or a habitual breaking and entering status offender, even if the magistrate is aware that the defendant's criminal record renders him or her eligible for such a charge. Further support for this recommendation comes from the fact that arrest warrants and magistrates' orders may be used only to charge "crimes";[53] the statutes in question define statuses, not crimes.[54] Finally, the relevant statutes refer only to charges in the form of an "indictment,"[55] adding additional support to the recommendation that charging decisions on habitual felon and related statuses must be made by the district attorney.

3. The Probable Cause Determination

a. Generally. Criminal process and pleadings require a finding of probable cause. With a citation, a law enforcement officer determines whether probable cause exists. For all other forms of criminal process and pleadings discussed in this publication, a judicial official determines whether probable cause exists.

b. Meaning of probable cause. To issue any of the forms of criminal process or pleadings discussed in this section, a magistrate must determine that there is probable cause to believe that a crime has been committed and that the person who has been arrested or who will be arrested or summoned committed that crime. The term "probable cause" does not have a precise definition.[56] The United States Supreme Court has instructed that all of the various definitions of probable cause boil down to this: a reasonable ground for belief of guilt.[57] Another shorthand definition that is sometimes used is "a fair probability."[58] However defined, the standard is less than proof beyond a reasonable doubt.[59]

In the context of issuing process, the probable cause determination involves a dual inquiry: whether there is a fair probability that (1) a crime was committed and (2) the person arrested or to be arrested or summoned committed the crime.[60] In order to find probable cause that an offense was committed, a magistrate must find probable cause for each element of the offense.

---

51. G.S. 14-7.3.

52. G.S. 14-7.28(a).

53. G.S. 15A-304 (arrest warrants), -511(c) (magistrates' orders).

54. *See, e.g.,* State v. Patton, 342 N.C. 633, 635 (1996) ("[b]eing an habitual felon is not a crime but rather a status").

55. G.S. 14-7.3, -7.9, -7.28.

56. Maryland v. Pringle, 540 U.S. 366, 371 (2003) ("The probable-cause standard is incapable of precise definition or quantification into percentages because it deals with probabilities and depends on the totality of the circumstances.").

57. *Id.* at 371.

58. Robert L. Farb, Arrest, Search, and Investigation in North Carolina 37 (UNC School of Government, 4th ed. 2011) (hereinafter Arrest, Search, and Investigation).

59. *Id.*

60. State v. Martin, 315 N.C. 667, 676 (1986).

c. Forms of evidence. The information establishing probable cause must be shown by one or more of the following:

- affidavit;
- oral testimony under oath or affirmation before the magistrate (e.g., by a law enforcement officer or a complaining witness);
- oral testimony under oath or affirmation presented by a law enforcement officer to a magistrate by means of an audio and video transmission in which both parties can see and hear each other; the procedure and equipment must be approved by the AOC based on a submission to the AOC by the senior resident superior court judge and the chief district court judge.[61]

As of this writing, the AOC has reported that twenty-three counties are approved for and are using video conferencing for this purpose. In counties where video conferencing is in place, magistrates should obtain and follow the local policy for use of such a technique.

d. Rules of evidence do not apply. When making a probable cause determination, a magistrate is not bound by the rules of evidence. Thus, hearsay that might be inadmissible at trial may be considered, provided it is reliable.[62]

e. Proper considerations in the probable cause determination

i. Totality of the circumstances

When considering whether there is probable cause to charge, a magistrate must consider the "totality of the circumstances."[63] While it is impossible to list all of the circumstances that might be relevant in every case that comes before a magistrate, some factors that might come into play include

- whether or not witnesses—including officers—are credible (see the section immediately below for a discussion of credibility);
- whether or not any physical evidence corroborates the story, e.g., bruises in an assault case;
- whether or not officers have corroborated information provided by witnesses;
- whether or not there is any scientific evidence;
- whether or not the defendant engaged in attempts to avoid detection or capture, such as flight and hiding evidence; and
- the experience level of the officer involved.

ii. Credibility

As noted above, one factor that should be considered in the probable cause determination is the credibility of witnesses.

ASSESSING CREDIBILITY—GENERALLY

As a general rule, when assessing credibility, a witness's story is more likely to be true if he or she

- has no history of lying or making false charges,
- is unbiased and has no motive to lie,
- provides a detailed statement, and
- is consistent in his or her story.

---

61. G.S. 15A-303(c); -304(d); -511(c).
62. Brinegar v. United States, 338 U.S. 160 (1949).
63. State v. Bullin, 150 N.C. App. 631, 638 (2002).

Although some case law supports consideration of a witness's demeanor in assessing credibility, magistrates should be careful about relying on factors such as nervousness and lack of eye contact, as these could easily be attributed to nervousness over the general situation or authority figures or cultural differences.

VICTIMS AND CITIZEN WITNESSES

Victims are persons harmed by crime, such as a person who is assaulted. Citizen witnesses are regular people who witness crime, such as a bystander who sees a robber flee after a convenience store robbery. Absent some reason to doubt the credibility of a victim or citizen witness, a magistrate may presume that a victim and a citizen witness are truthful.[64]

CONFIDENTIAL INFORMANTS

A confidential informant is one whose identity is known to officers but not revealed when the statement of probable cause is provided. When making the probable cause determination, a magistrate may not presume that a confidential informant is truthful. To establish truthfulness of a confidential informant's information, the officer typically will provide the magistrate with facts indicating (1) the basis for the informant's information (e.g., that the informant personally observed the defendant doing the illegal act) and (2) the informant's credibility or the reliability of the information.[65] The second showing typically is made by facts indicating the officer's track record with the informant or the officer's corroboration of the informant's information.[66] Note that an officer's conclusory statement that an informant is reliable is not sufficient.[67]

ANONYMOUS TIPSTERS

An anonymous tip is a lead from someone whose identity is unknown. Rarely—if ever—will an anonymous tip by itself provide probable cause.[68] However, an anonymous tip can contribute to probable cause if it is reliable.[69] In a recent U.S. Supreme Court case, the Court held to be reliable an anonymous 911 call reporting that the driver of a specified pickup forced the caller off the road.[70] The Court found the tip reliable where the tipster explained the basis of her knowledge (she experienced the event in question), the tip was contemporaneous with the event (officers corroborated that the vehicle was where it should be based on the caller's information about the vehicle's direction of travel and the time elapsed between the call and the officer's location of the vehicle on the road), and it was made through the 911 system.[71] Some North Carolina case law suggests that a witness whose anonymity has been placed at risk by providing the tip should normally be treated as a citizen witness, not an anonymous tipster.[72]

---

64. United States v. DeQuasie, 373 F.3d 509, 523 & n.21 (4th Cir. 2004); Easton v. City of Boulder, 776 F.2d 1441, 1449 (10th Cir. 1985); Arrest, Search, and Investigation at 378–79.

65. Arrest, Search, and Investigation at 379–81.

66. Arrest, Search, and Investigation at 380.

67. State v. Hughes, 353 N.C. 200, 204 (2000).

68. Navarette v. California, 134 S. Ct. 1683, 1688 (2014). *Navarette* was a vehicle stop case involving the reasonable suspicion standard. Given that the Court determined that an anonymous tip alone rarely will provide reasonable suspicion, such a source is even more unlikely to satisfy the higher probable cause standard.

69. *Id.*

70. *Id.*

71. *Id.*

72. State v. Maready, 362 N.C. 614, 619–20 (2008). *But see Navarette*, 134 S. Ct. 1683 (treating a tip as anonymous even though it was made to the 911 system, which generally has recording and caller identification features); State v. Blankenship, ___ N.C. App. ___, 748 S.E.2d 616, 618 (2013) (tipster who called

f. Improper considerations. When making the probable cause determination, a magistrate should not be influenced by the fact that the defendant is already in custody. Nor should a magistrate consider, as a general rule, application of the exclusionary rule (such as the legality of an arrest or search).[73] There are several reasons for this rule. First, magistrates are not trained in the complex law of search and seizure or in the law regarding whether a defendant has standing to raise such a constitutional question. Also, no lawyer representing the State is present at the initial appearance to explain why the evidence may have been obtained legally. There are established procedures for a defendant to raise any issues regarding the constitutionality of an arrest, search, or seizure. However, all of these procedures apply in trial court, not before the magistrate. Finally, when making the probable cause determination, a magistrate should not—as a general rule—consider whether the defendant has a defense to the crime. One exception to this rule might be where a misdemeanor is alleged and the two-year statute of limitations clearly applies.[74] Another might be a domestic violence situation where self-defense justifies one party's actions.

4. Charging Language

Once a magistrate has identified the relevant criminal offense and determined that there is probable cause to charge, the magistrate must prepare the appropriate criminal process or pleading. Except for an OFA, all criminal process and pleadings issued by a magistrate—criminal summons, warrant for arrest, and magistrate's order—must include charging language.

A magistrate can find the appropriate charging language in one of two places. When issuing criminal process through NCAWARE, generic charging language will appear automatically when the offense is entered in the computer. For times when the computer system is not operating, charging language can be found in JEFFREY B. WELTY, ARREST WARRANT AND INDICTMENT FORMS (UNC School of Government, 6th ed. 2010) (hereinafter ARREST WARRANT AND INDICTMENT FORMS). Neither NCAWARE nor ARREST WARRANT AND INDICTMENT FORMS includes all North Carolina offenses that might be charged. If the facts presented do not fit into the charging language for the included offenses, the magistrate should not force the form language to fit the circumstances but rather modify the form language to fit the facts or draft new language. For offenses not included in ARREST WARRANT AND INDICTMENT FORMS, the magistrate will need to draft charging language based on the relevant statute. When doing this, it is best to track the statutory language exactly, adding in factual details as necessary based on the particular situation presented. See section I.B.9, below, for general guidelines. For a quick listing of most criminal offenses in North Carolina, magistrates can consult the contents at the beginning of Chapter 14 in NORTH CAROLINA CRIMINAL LAW AND PROCEDURE (LexisNexis 2013) (the "red book" provided annually to all magistrates by the AOC) or the table of contents in NORTH CAROLINA CRIMES, which the AOC purchases for all magistrates.

---

911 from his cell phone was treated as an anonymous tipster even though the 911 call operator was able to use the caller's cell phone number to identify him).

73. *See* United States v. Calandra, 414 U.S. 338, 344–45 (1974) (a grand jury may consider evidence obtained illegally; "the validity of an indictment is not affected by the character of the evidence considered").

74. See section I.B.5 (discussing the statute of limitations for misdemeanors).

5. Statute of Limitations

There is a two-year statute of limitations for misdemeanors.[75] This means that valid process must be issued within two years of the completion of the misdemeanor. There is no statute of limitations for felonies.[76] This means that there is no outer limit on the time when process may be issued for a felony.

6. Venue

a. Generally. When a magistrate issues a criminal summons, arrest warrant, or OFA, it is valid throughout the state.[77] For good reason, however, arrest warrants (and other forms of process) usually are issued only for crimes committed in the magistrate's own county. The reason for this informal rule is that a person will be tried in the county where the charged offense occurred (venue).[78] Thus, if a magistrate from county A issues arrest warrants for crimes committed in county B, the defendant and all the paperwork will need to be transferred to county B for the trial.

b. Concurrent venue. G.S. 15A-131(e) states that an offense "occurs in a county if any act . . . constituting part of the offense occurs within the territorial limits of the county." If acts constituting part of the offense occur in more than one county (for example, a worthless check written in one county and mailed to another county), each county has venue to conduct the trial.[79] Put another way, the two counties have concurrent venue. If counties have concurrent venue, the first county in which a criminal process is issued has exclusive venue.[80]

c. Venue for rape or sexual offenses. G.S. 15A-136 is a special venue statute that applies when a defendant transports a person for the purpose of committing a rape, sexual offense, or sexual battery and commits one of those offenses. Under G.S. 15A-136, venue is in any county where the transportation began, continued, or ended.

d. Venue for initial and first appearance. Although venue for initial appearance before a magistrate may be anywhere, venue for first appearance before a district court judge in a felony case must be in a judicial district that contains the county where the felony occurred.[81]

7. Transmittal of Out-of-County Process

As noted above, if a crime has been committed in county A and the defendant lives in county B, a magistrate in county A may issue criminal process for the crime. Process created in the NCAWARE system in county A can be printed out in county B and serve as an original document for the purpose of service.[82] However, there may be circumstances when a magistrate in county A wants to have a paper copy of the process delivered to county B along with recommendations for conditions of release. Form AOC-CR-236 should be used in such a case. The form has a space where a magistrate may recommend conditions for release. However, this is only a recommendation, and it does not have to be followed. When using this form, magistrates should be sure to include the court date in their county because the magistrate in the arresting county may not know the originating county's court dates.

---

75. G.S. 15-1.
76. State v. Johnson, 275 N.C. 264, 271 (1969).
77. G.S. 15A-303(f) (summons); -304(f) (warrant); -305(d) (OFA).
78. G.S. 15A-131(a).
79. G.S. 15A-132(a).
80. G.S. 15A-132(c).
81. G.S. 15A-131(b) & (f).
82. G.S. 15A-101.1(5) & (9)b; -301.1(f).

Table 2.   Basic Pleading Rules

Defendant's Name	• A criminal pleading must contain the name or other identification of the defendant. G.S. 15A-924(a)(1).
	• If the defendant's name is unknown, you do not have to use "John Doe"; you can give a detailed physical description of the defendant and his or her address, if known.
	• If the defendant's aliases are known they can be used. State v. Taylor, 61 N.C. App. 589, 591 (1983).
Witnesses	• Complaining witnesses are witnesses who give testimony under oath; a complaining witness can be a victim, an officer, a friend or relative of a victim, or any other person who has information about the alleged crime and gives testimony under oath.
	• People who give statements that are not under oath (e.g., to an officer at the scene) should be listed as witnesses but not as complaining witnesses.
Separate Counts	• A pleading must contain a separate count for each charged offense; allegations in one count may be incorporated by reference in another count. G.S. 15A-924(a)(2).
County	• Each count must contain a statement or cross-reference indicating the county in which the charged offense was committed. G.S. 15A-924(a)(3).
Offense Date	• Each count must contain a statement or cross-reference indicating on or about what date the offense occurred. G.S. 15A-924(a)(4). The phrase "on or about" appears on the printed forms when the paperwork is created in the NCAWARE system and is on all hard copy AOC forms.
Factual Statement	• Each count must contain a plain and concise statement asserting facts supporting every element of the offense and the charge that the defendant committed the offense. G.S. 15A-924(a)(5).
	• The offense must be charged with sufficient certainty so that the defendant may prepare a defense. *Id.*
	• The standard charging language serves as this factual statement. See section I.B.4, above, for a discussion of charging language.
Law Violated	• Each count must cite the statute, rule, regulation, ordinance, or other provision alleged to have been violated. G.S. 15A-924(a)(6).
	• If a city or county ordinance violation is alleged, the pleading must cite the section number and caption (e.g., "Sec. 5-20, Letting chickens run loose prohibited"). If the ordinance is not codified, the caption must be pleaded. The last form in Arrest Warrant and Indictment Forms provides an example of charging language to use in this situation.
Miscellaneous Issues	• Do not use abbreviations (such as "a/d/w" with "IK" or "ccw"). The abbreviation might be clear to you but not to others.
	• If you have to prepare process for an offense for which there is no standard charging language, avoid using the word "or" when describing the ways the offense was committed; instead use the word "and" (e.g., confine, restrain, and remove).
	• The word "feloniously" must appear in a pleading that charges a felony. However, use of that word in a misdemeanor pleading will be considered harmless surplusage.
	• When naming businesses in criminal pleadings refer to the formal name of the business, not its common name; that is, be sure to include "inc.," "corp.," "ltd.," and so forth (e.g., "Roses Stores, Inc.," not "Roses Store"). If you have a question about the proper name of a North Carolina corporation, you can search for that information on the North Carolina secretary of state's website, www.secretary.state.nc.us/corporations/csearch.aspx.
	• For information on charging fugitives from other states, see section IV, below.

Table 3. Magistrate's Recall of Process

Type of Process	By Whom?	When?	Recall Allowed/ Required?
Citation	No one	Never	No
Warrant	Issuing official or person authorized to act for such official	(1) Before defendant has been served and (2) No probable cause for issuance	Required
Summons	Issuing official or person authorized to act for such official	(1) Before defendant has been served and (2) No probable cause for issuance	Required
OFA	Judicial official in trial division where issued or person authorized to act for that official	(1) Before defendant has been served and (2) Good cause is shown, including that • a copy of the process has been served on the defendant; • all relevant charges have been disposed of; • the defendant did not commit the charged offense; or • grounds for issuing the OFA did not exist, no longer exist, or have been satisfied.	Allowed

Source: G.S. 15A-301(g).

8. Service of Criminal Process

Criminal process must be served on the defendant.[83] Note that law enforcement officers are authorized to make an arrest without having the actual warrant or OFA in hand, provided they have knowledge that it has been issued and not executed (such as a DCI message).[84] Although the warrant or OFA—like all criminal process—must be served on the defendant, the arrest itself is valid without service.

9. Requirements for Criminal Pleadings

As noted in section I, above, the citation, criminal summons, warrant for arrest, and magistrate's order serve as the state's pleading in certain criminal cases. The requirements for valid pleadings, set out in G.S. 15A-924, are specific and technical. It is important that magistrates follow these requirements along with other helpful pleading rules, all of which are listed in Table 2.

C. Recall of Process

Sometimes it becomes necessary to recall process, such as when a magistrate learns that the wrong person was identified as a perpetrator. Recall of process is governed by G.S. 15A-301(g). The relevant rules are summarized in Table 3. Unless specifically directed to do so, a magistrate should never recall process issued by a judge. When a magistrate recalls process, the magistrate must enter the recall into NCAWARE.[85]

---

83. G.S. 15A-301(c).
84. G.S. 15A-401(a)(2).
85. G.S. 15A-301(g).

II. The Initial Appearance

The initial appearance is a defendant's first contact with the judicial system. Every person who is arrested must appear before a judicial official for an initial appearance. This section describes the procedure for conducting an initial appearance. This procedure applies in all cases except those in which a magistrate is authorized to dispose of the matter under G.S. 7A-273 (magistrate can accept guilty pleas for certain infractions and misdemeanors).[86]

A. Initial Appearance—Basic Procedure

Figure 1 illustrates the basic procedure for conducting an initial appearance. The subsections that follow flesh out some additional details about that procedure as well as note exceptions to it.

B. Timing of the Initial Appearance

1. Generally: Without Unnecessary Delay

A law enforcement officer must take a person arrested (with or without a warrant or an OFA) before a judicial official *without unnecessary delay.*[87]

2. Exceptions: When the Initial Appearance May Be Delayed

In some situations it is necessary to delay the initial appearance. The sections below discuss when a delay of the initial appearance is permissible. Later sections of this publication discuss when a magistrate holds the initial appearance but delays setting conditions[88] and when a defendant's release may be delayed even after he or she has satisfied conditions of pretrial release.[89]

    a. Reasonable delay to determine conditions. As has been noted, the initial appearance must be held without unnecessary delay. The period required for a magistrate to do a timely and reasonable investigation into the facts relevant to a pretrial release decision is a necessary delay.

    b. Defendants who refuse to identify themselves. Sometimes a defendant brought before a magistrate for an initial appearance will refuse to identify himself or herself. Without knowing a defendant's identity, it is impossible for a magistrate to determine what conditions of pretrial release should be imposed. The magistrate will not be able to determine, among other things, whether the defendant has a record, has previously failed to appear, or what connections the defendant has with the community that are relevant to a risk of flight. When this happens, and there is no written local

---

86. G.S. 15A-511(a)(2).
87. G.S. 15A-501(2), -511(a)(1).
88. See section III.B.2.
89. See section III.F.2.

Figure 1.   Initial Appearance Procedure for Magistrates

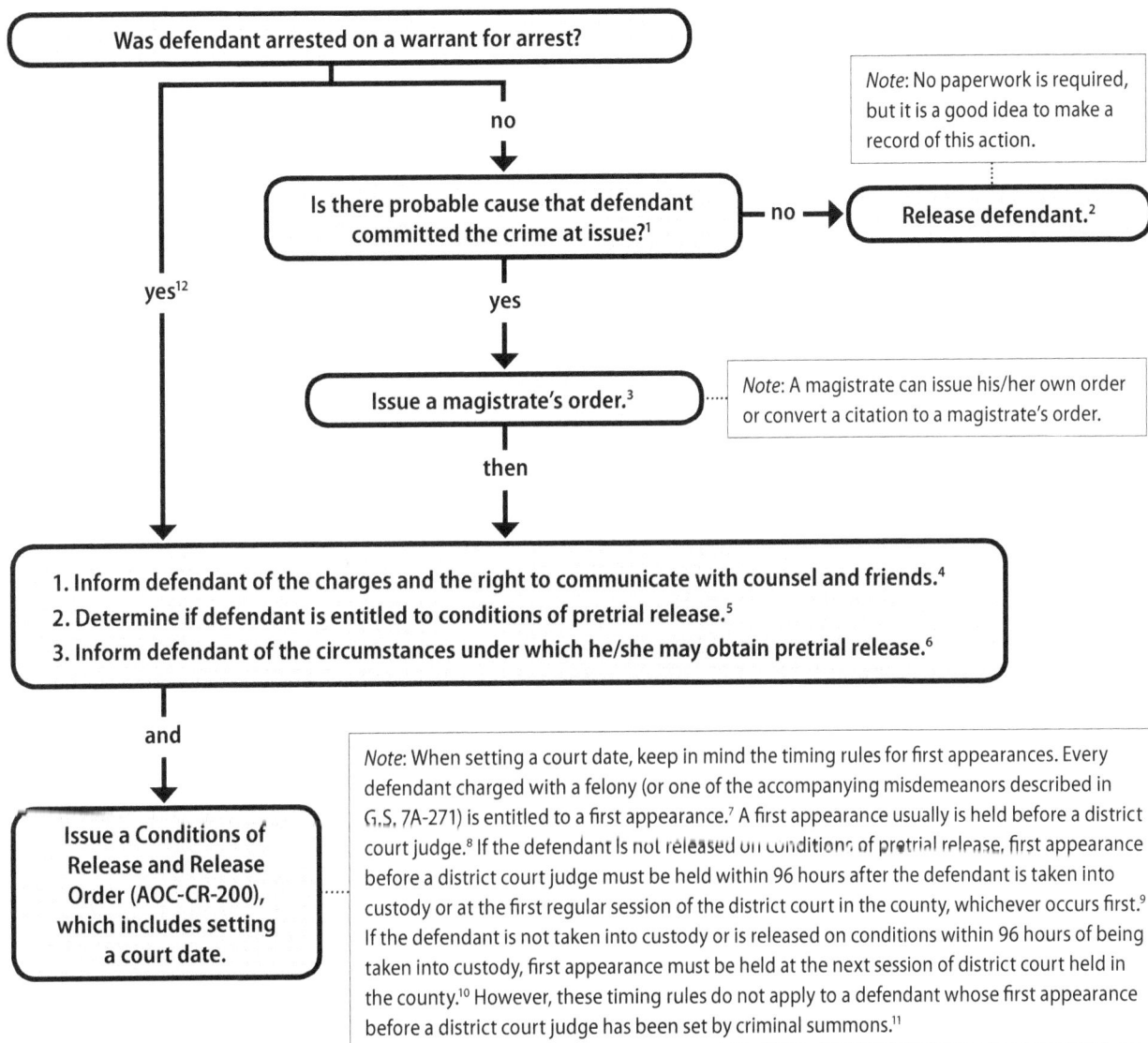

```
┌─────────────────────────────────────────────────┐
│  Was defendant arrested on a warrant for arrest?  │
└─────────────────────────────────────────────────┘
         │                         │
       yes[12]                    no
         │                         ▼
         │            ┌──────────────────────────────┐     no     ┌──────────────────────┐
         │            │ Is there probable cause that  │ ─────────▶ │  Release defendant.[2] │
         │            │ defendant committed the       │            └──────────────────────┘
         │            │ crime at issue?[1]            │
         │            └──────────────────────────────┘
         │                         │
         │                        yes
         │                         ▼
         │            ┌──────────────────────────────┐
         │            │   Issue a magistrate's order.[3]│
         │            └──────────────────────────────┘
         │                         │
         │                        then
         │                         ▼
```

Note: No paperwork is required, but it is a good idea to make a record of this action.

Note: A magistrate can issue his/her own order or convert a citation to a magistrate's order.

┌───┐
│ 1. Inform defendant of the charges and the right to communicate with counsel and friends.[4] │
│ 2. Determine if defendant is entitled to conditions of pretrial release.[5]   │
│ 3. Inform defendant of the circumstances under which he/she may obtain pretrial release.[6] │
└───┘

and

┌──────────────────────────┐
│ Issue a Conditions of   │
│ Release and Release   │
│ Order (AOC-CR-200),   │
│ which includes setting   │
│ a court date.   │
└──────────────────────────┘

Note: When setting a court date, keep in mind the timing rules for first appearances. Every defendant charged with a felony (or one of the accompanying misdemeanors described in G.S. 7A-271) is entitled to a first appearance.[7] A first appearance usually is held before a district court judge.[8] If the defendant is not released on conditions of pretrial release, first appearance before a district court judge must be held within 96 hours after the defendant is taken into custody or at the first regular session of the district court in the county, whichever occurs first.[9] If the defendant is not taken into custody or is released on conditions within 96 hours of being taken into custody, first appearance must be held at the next session of district court held in the county.[10] However, these timing rules do not apply to a defendant whose first appearance before a district court judge has been set by criminal summons.[11]

---

1. G.S. 15A-511(c)(1).
2. G.S. 15A-511(c)(2).
3. G.S. 15A-511(c)(3).
4. G.S. 15A-511(b). Note that G.S. 7A-146(11) and -292(15) authorize chief district judges to give magistrates who are duly licensed attorneys the authority to appoint counsel for defendants entitled to counsel at state expense. In making appointments, magistrates must follow the rules adopted by the Office of Indigent Defense Services. *See* G.S. 7A-452(a) (upon a determination that a person is indigent and entitled to counsel under Article 36 of G.S. Chapter 7A, counsel shall be appointed in accordance with rules adopted by IDS).
5. See section III below, discussing conditions of pretrial release.
6. G.S. 15A-511(b).
7. G.S. 15A-601(a).
8. *Id.*
9. G.S. 15A-601(c).
10. *Id.*
11. *Id.*
12. A magistrate does not need to make a finding of probable cause during an initial appearance for an arrest with a warrant because probable cause already was found when the process was issued. For this same reason, a magistrate's order is not needed; the warrant for arrest serves as the criminal pleading.

procedure that applies, the magistrate has a couple of options. Note that if this issue consistently arises in the county and there is no written policy addressing it, the magistrate may want to ask the senior resident superior court judge or chief district court judge for a written policy or other formal advice so that all magistrates can respond to this problem in a consistent manner.

First, it seems reasonable to delay the initial appearance while a law enforcement officer completes an investigation into the defendant's identity. Such an investigation may not be feasible in all cases, particularly when the crime is not a serious one. Note, however, that if a person (1) is charged with an offense involving impaired driving, as defined in G.S. 20-4.01(24a), or driving while license revoked when the revocation is for an impaired driving revocation, as defined in G.S. 20-28.2, and (2) the person cannot be identified by a valid form of identification, the arresting officer must have the person fingerprinted and photographed.[90] This requirement does not necessarily result in an identification of the person, but it does impose additional duties on law enforcement. If the magistrate delays the initial appearance to allow the officer to investigate and the officer's investigation is unsuccessful or cannot be done quickly, the magistrate should consider the other option set out below; magistrates should not allow an indefinite delay of the initial appearance.

A second option for dealing with a defendant who refuses to identify himself or herself is to hold the initial appearance, set conditions in light of the potential flight risk associated with a person who will not identify himself or herself, and include as a condition of pretrial release either that the defendant adequately identify himself or herself or that an adequate identification of the defendant has otherwise been determined.

Note that regardless of which procedure is used, it is probably not permissible, and it is not advisable, to require a defendant to produce a United States government–issued picture identification. This is because no law requires people to have such a form of identification, and some may not have it. Also, any reasonable form of identification may be satisfactory even if the defendant does not have any written form of identification—for example, when a responsible member of the community vouches for the defendant's identity.

Procedures for dealing with noncitizens are discussed in section II.H, below.

c. Defendants who are unruly, intoxicated, etc. Under G.S. 15A-511(a)(3) a magistrate may delay the initial appearance and order a defendant confined without bond for a "reasonable time" if the defendant, when brought before the magistrate,

- is so unruly that the defendant disrupts and impedes the proceedings,
- becomes unconscious,
- is grossly intoxicated, or
- is otherwise unable to understand his or her procedural rights (for example, the defendant needs a sign language interpreter).

The purpose of this delay is not to punish the defendant but simply to postpone the process until the defendant can understand his or her rights.

The procedure for delaying the initial appearance in these circumstances is described in Table 4.

Magistrates should not confuse the statutory authorization to delay discussed above—for example, when the defendant is too intoxicated to understand his or her rights—with an impaired driving hold. In the situations addressed in this section, the initial appearance is delayed because

---

90. G.S. 15A-502(a2).

Table 4. Procedure for Delaying Initial Appearance When Defendant Is Unruly, Etc.

1. Decide whether to delay before beginning the initial appearance.	• In some circumstances you might not realize that one of the statutory reasons for delay is at issue until the initial appearance has begun. For example, the defendant may not become unruly until then. If this happens, stop the proceeding and continue as outlined below.
2. For cooling off, use a holding cell or a bench in the magistrate's office.	• If the defendant simply is being disruptive and needs to cool off, you can order an officer to place the defendant in a holding cell for a short period of time, such as twenty minutes, or, if there is no holding cell, have the officer supervise the defendant on a bench in the magistrate's office.
3. Use the release order to confine the defendant to jail.	• If you order the defendant confined to jail, you must use the release order, AOC-CR-200, to do so. Never commit a defendant to jail without a written order.
	• When using the release order to commit the defendant to jail, only complete the "Order of Commitment" portion of form. Do not complete the upper portion of the release order concerning conditions of release. Because the initial appearance is being delayed, conditions should not be determined at this time. If the upper portion of the release order is completed, the defendant must be released if he or she satisfies the conditions. G.S. 15A-537. That is true regardless of what directions are given under the order of commitment (except for impaired driving detentions, discussed in section III.F.2.b, below).
	• Check only the box entitled "hold him/her for the following purpose." The purpose listed will vary according to the reason that the defendant is confined. If the defendant is simply disruptive, you can direct the jailer to "hold defendant until defendant is calm and agrees not to disrupt the proceedings." If the defendant is grossly intoxicated, you can direct the jailer to "hold defendant until sober enough to understand rights."
	• In all cases, check regularly with the jailer about the defendant's condition. Do not leave complete discretion with a jailer to determine when the defendant is ready for his or her initial appearance. It is your responsibility—not the jailer's—to determine whether the defendant is ready for his or her initial appearance.
	• Always put an outer time limit on the confinement. G.S. 15A-511(a)(3) (magistrates' order delaying the initial appearance "must provide for an initial appearance within a reasonable time").
4. A defendant may be brought back before a different magistrate for the initial appearance.	• The second magistrate is not modifying the first magistrate's release order but, rather, is changing the order of commitment, which is expressly allowed by G.S. 15A-521(b) (order of commitment may be modified "by the same or another judicial official"). Conditions should never have been set, and therefore they are being determined for the first time.
5. After the defendant is returned, conduct the initial appearance and set conditions as usual.	• See section III, below (discussing pretrial release conditions).

the defendant's condition prevents the defendant from understanding the proceeding. The impaired driving hold, meanwhile, discussed in section III.F.2.b, below, comes into play only when the defendant is sober enough that the magistrate can conduct the initial appearance, and it serves a different purpose (to prevent injury to persons and property) from that of the statutorily authorized delay discussed here.

d. Defendants requiring hospital care. In some cases an arrested defendant will require immediate hospital care. When this happens, it is appropriate to delay the initial appearance until the defendant is released from the hospital. Such a delay is not considered unnecessary.[91] Except for implied consent offenses,[92] it does not appear that a magistrate has the authority to hold the initial appearance in the hospital. The statutes specifically authorize magistrates to hold initial appearances for implied consent offenses anywhere in the county[93] but are silent as to this issue with respect to all other offenses. This leads to the inference that "out-of-office" initial appearances are authorized only for implied consent offenses. As a practical matter, this means that the arresting authority must maintain custody of the defendant until the initial appearance occurs; officers cannot "unarrest" a person simply because it turns out that the hospital stay will be lengthy or expensive.

e. Out-of-county pickups from neighboring counties. In some cases a defendant will be arrested for a crime occurring in a neighboring county. If officers from the neighboring county verify that they are coming immediately to pick up the defendant and transport him or her for an initial appearance in that county, it may be appropriate to delay the initial appearance in order for this transfer to occur. However, there is some question about whether or not this delay is "unnecessary." Therefore, magistrates should not delay the initial appearance unless they are certain that the delay will be short and that the officers from the neighboring county are on their way. Magistrates are advised not to delay if officers from the neighboring county make vague statements about when they will be coming (e.g., "at some time," "as soon as possible") to get the defendant.

C. Defendant's Presence

The defendant must be present at the initial appearance.[94]

D. Audio and Video Transmission and Videoconferencing

An initial appearance for noncapital offenses may be conducted through an audio and video transmission that allows the magistrate (or other judicial official) and the defendant to see and hear each other.[95] If the defendant has counsel, the defendant must be allowed to communicate

---

91. State v. Brown, 233 Ariz. 153, 159 (Ct. App. 2013) (defendant's hospitalization excused the delay in conducting the initial appearance; citing cases from other jurisdictions "holding that delay arising from a need to provide the accused with medical treatment is excusable under their respective rules requiring an initial appearance without unnecessary delay").

92. See section II.J, below (defining implied consent offenses and discussing initial appearance procedure for these offenses).

93. G.S. 20-38.4(a)(1).

94. G.S. 15A-511.

95. G.S. 15A-511(a1).

fully and confidentially with counsel during the proceeding.[96] The procedure and equipment must be approved by the AOC, based on a submission to the AOC by the senior regular resident superior court judge and the chief district court judge.[97] As of this writing, the AOC has reported that twenty-two counties are equipped to conduct initial appearances in this manner.

E. Federal Offenses

A magistrate may hold an initial appearance for a person arrested for a federal offense.[98] Conditions of pretrial release are determined according to federal law.

F. Appointing Counsel

Magistrates who are licensed attorneys may be designated by their chief district court judge to appoint counsel pursuant to G.S. Chapter 7A, Article 36.[99] However, such magistrates may not appoint counsel for potentially capital offenses, as defined by rules adopted by the Office of Indigent Defense Services, or accept waivers of counsel.[100] Any magistrate who has been so designated should get guidance from his or her chief district court judge on when the counsel appointment should be made, the procedure to be followed, and how to determine indigency.

G. Non-English-Speaking Defendants

When a non-English-speaking defendant is brought before a magistrate for an initial appearance, the magistrate should use the telephone interpreting services, installed by the AOC's Court Services Division, to ensure that the defendant understands the proceedings and his or her rights. As of this writing, the AOC Court Services Division has implemented telephone interpreting services in all magistrates' offices.

> *Practice Pointer*: For information about or training on the AOC's telephone interpreting services, contact Kellie Meyers, Court Management Specialist, Office of Language Access Service, North Carolina Administrative Office of the Courts, (919) 890-1214.

H. Noncitizens

In recent years a number of issues have arisen about magistrates' authority to hold defendants for a variety of immigration-related issues. It is important to note at the outset that a magistrate has no authority to hold an arrestee simply because he or she is not a U.S. citizen.

---

96. *Id.*
97. *Id.*
98. 18 U.S.C. § 3041.
99. G.S. 7A-146(11).
100. *Id.*

G.S. 162-62(a) provides that whenever a person charged with a felony or an impaired driving offense is confined to a jail or a local confinement facility, the person in charge of the facility must attempt to determine if the prisoner is a legal resident of the United States by questioning the person and/or examining documents. If the prisoner's status cannot be determined, the person in charge must, if possible, make an inquiry of Immigration and Customs Enforcement (ICE) of the United States Department of Homeland Security.[101] However, the law imposing these requirements expressly states that it cannot be construed to deny bond to a prisoner or to prevent the prisoner from being released from confinement when the prisoner is otherwise eligible for release.[102]

Although a magistrate may not hold a defendant simply because he or she is not a U.S. citizen, citizenship status may be relevant in determining conditions of pretrial release, such as when the arrestee has no contacts in the community and was planning to return to his or her home country in the near future, thus creating a flight risk. How such factors play into the magistrate's determination of the conditions of pretrial release is discussed in section III.C.3, below.

Another immigration issue sometimes arises when the arresting officer tells the magistrate that there is an ICE detainer or that ICE is "interested" in the defendant. Although ICE has many functions, one of its responsibilities is detaining and removing noncitizens who are in the country illegally. An ICE detainer refers to a document issued by ICE, frequently to a local jail, asking the jailer to hold a person for up to forty-eight hours after the person would otherwise be released so that ICE can take custody of that person. For example, suppose a defendant is in jail on a $5,000 secured bond. Normally, when the defendant is able to make that bond he or she must be released. However, if an ICE detainer is in place, the jailer will hold the defendant for up to forty-eight hours after the defendant makes bond so that ICE can take custody.

When an officer brings a defendant to a magistrate and an ICE detainer is in place, the magistrate should follow the normal procedure for conducting the initial appearance and setting conditions of pretrial release. There is no special hold to implement, and the magistrate is not authorized to hold the defendant. The detainer is in place, and if the defendant meets his or her conditions of pretrial release the jail will hold the defendant per the detainer. However, the fact that a detainer is in place may affect the magistrate's decision about appropriate conditions; for example, if the defendant is facing deportation, there may be a flight risk.

Likewise, when an officer brings a defendant to a magistrate and states that ICE is "interested" or is "investigating whether a detainer should issue," the magistrate should follow normal procedures for conducting an initial appearance and setting conditions of pretrial release. There is no special hold to implement, and the magistrate is not authorized to hold the defendant for this purpose. However, in this situation the magistrate may learn of facts that will be relevant to his or her determination regarding the appropriate conditions of pretrial release.

Procedures for dealing with defendants who refuse to identify themselves are discussed in section II.B.2.b, above.

---

101. G.S.162-62(b).
102. G.S.162-62(c).

I. "Paperless Arrests"

Law enforcement officers may make arrests without having the actual warrant or OFA in hand, provided that they have knowledge that it has been issued and not executed.[103] This publication refers to such arrests as "paperless arrests," which are valid in North Carolina, even for out-of-county process. When an officer brings a defendant before a magistrate on a paperless arrest, the magistrate should not release the defendant simply because the officer cannot provide the paperwork.

With the implementation of NCAWARE, issues with paperless arrests are becoming a thing of the past. This is because all warrants and OFAs are now in NCAWARE and a printed copy of a document created in NCAWARE constitutes an original.[104] Thus, a paperless arrest can be "converted" to an arrest with a warrant simply by printing out a copy of the warrant or OFA from the computer. If the paperwork is not in NCAWARE, a faxed copy constitutes an original.[105]

If a defendant is brought in on a paperless arrest and the warrant or OFA is no longer outstanding—because, for example, it has been recalled—the magistrate should release the person without holding an initial appearance or setting release conditions. Also, the magistrate should notify authorities of the erroneous information so that the person will not be rearrested. The magistrate may choose to have the officer do this.

If the warrant or OFA is valid, the magistrate should investigate appropriate pretrial release conditions, including in the case of out-of-county charges, contacting the other county for information. Although the initial appearance must be conducted without unnecessary delay, the law allows the magistrate time to make a reasonable investigation regarding pretrial release conditions.[106] However, the magistrate may not delay the initial appearance because officers from the other county say they will be coming at some time to get the defendant. The law requires the magistrate to hold the initial appearance without unnecessary delay.[107] Magistrates should proceed with the initial appearance unless the officers are from a nearby county and can *quickly* pick up the defendant for an initial appearance in the originating county. Thus, except for a possible reasonable delay to investigate pretrial release conditions for out-of-county defendants, the initial appearance for a paperless arrest is conducted just like any other initial appearance. Note that when setting conditions, magistrates have no authority to hold a defendant for service of criminal process.

If a magistrate needs to get a court date for an out-of-county officer, that information can be obtained by doing a Statewide Officer Court Appearance Query on the AOC web page, www1.aoc.state.nc.us/www/calendars/OfficerQuery.html (see Figure 2).

J. Implied Consent Cases

The sections above discuss the basic procedure for conducting the initial appearance. This section discusses several special procedures that apply in implied consent offenses, which are listed in Table 5.

---

103. G.S. 15A-401(a)(2).
104. G.S. 15A-101.1(5) & (9)b; -301.1(f).
105. G.S. 15A-101.1(9)a.
106. See section II.B.2.a, above (discussing delay for this reason).
107. See section II.B.1, above.

Figure 2.   Screen Shot from North Carolina Administrative Office of the Courts Web Page for Statewide Officer Court Appearance Query

THE NORTH CAROLINA COURT SYSTEM

Judicial Directory | Judicial Forms | Frequently Asked Questions | Search | Contact Us

CITIZENS
COURTS   COURTS
EMPLOYEES

- Calendars Home
- Civil Calendars
- Civil Calendar Attorney Query by Bar Number
- Criminal Calendars
- Citation Query by Citation Number
- Citation Query by Defendant Name
- District and Superior Court Query
- Impaired Driving Query
- *Statewide Officer Court Appearance Query*
- Superior Court Master Calendar
- Calendar FAQ's
- Contacts by County
- Criminal Calendar Code Definitions
- Judicial Branch Holiday Schedule

Statewide Officer Court Appearance Query

The following methods can be used to search the Officer's Court Appearance database:

- You may use a combination of County, Agency, Office's Last Name and Officer Number.
  (When entering the Officer's Last Name, enter the last name followed by a comma, no space, and first initial. If you use only the first name, it will produce incomplete results.)
  For example, John Smith could be entered Smith or Smith,J

- You may use "All Agencies" or "All Counties" and an officer's last name and/or officer number.

- You must select a specific County or Agency when leaving the Officer Name and Officer Number blank.

- Note: Officer Numbers might not be unique between Agencies or Counties.

County: [ALL Counties   ‡]

Agency: [ALL Agencies   ‡]

Officer Name: [   ]

Officer Number: [   ]   **NEW!**

        Search   Reset

Query data may be up to 24 hours old.

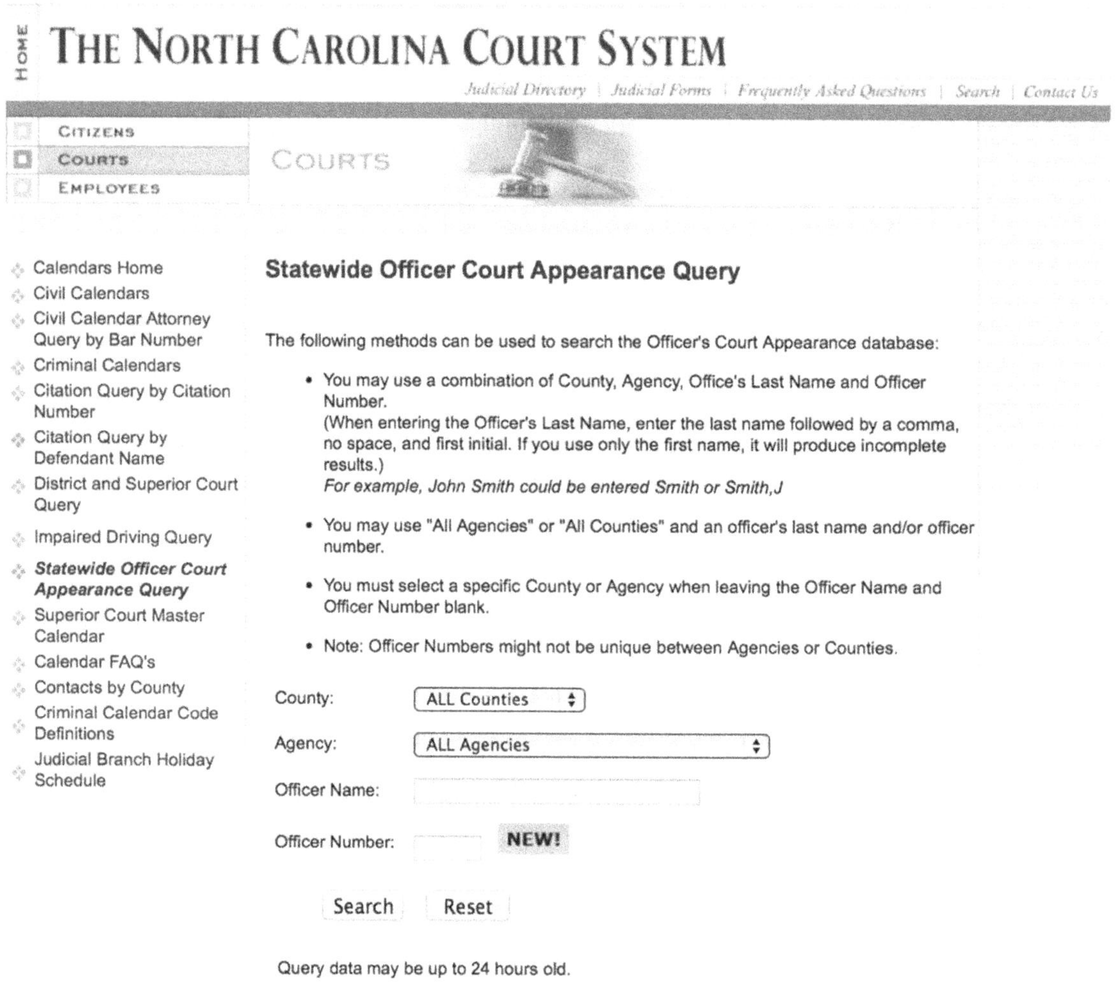

1. Chemical Analyses, etc., May Be Done Prior to the Initial Appearance

G.S. 20-38.3 provides, in part, that a law enforcement officer must take a person arrested for an implied consent offense to a judicial official for an initial appearance after completing all investigatory procedures, crash reports, chemical analyses, and related procedures.[108] Before this provision was enacted, there was some question as to whether completing these tasks before the initial appearance violated the rule that the initial appearance must be held without unnecessary delay.[109] This statute makes it clear that the officer must complete these tasks before the initial appearance.

---

108. G.S. 20-38.3(5).
109. See section II.B.1, above.

Table 5. Implied Consent Offenses

1. Impaired driving under G.S. 20-138.1
2. Impaired driving in a commercial vehicle under G.S. 20-138.2
3. Habitual impaired driving under G.S. 20-138.5
4. Any death by vehicle or serious injury by vehicle offense under G.S. 20-141.4, when based on impaired driving or a substantially similar offense under previous law
5. First- or second-degree murder under G.S. 14-17 or involuntary manslaughter under G.S. 14-18, when based on impaired driving
6. Driving by person under twenty-one after consuming alcohol or drugs under G.S. 20-138.3
7. Violating no-alcohol condition of limited privilege under G.S. 20-179.3
8. Impaired instruction under G.S. 20-12.1
9. Operating commercial motor vehicle after consuming alcohol under G.S. 20-138.2A
10. Operating school bus, school activity bus, or child care vehicle after consuming alcohol under G.S. 20-138.2B
11. Transporting open container of alcoholic beverage under G.S. 20-138.7(a)
12. Certain violations of restriction requiring ignition interlock under G.S. 20-17.8(f)

Source: G.S. 20-16.2(a1); -4.01(24a).

2. Initial Appearance May Be Held Anywhere in County

A magistrate may hold an initial appearance for an implied consent offense anywhere in the county.[110] The relevant statute provides that a magistrate "shall, to the extent practicable, be available at locations other than the courthouse when it will expedite the initial appearance."[111] This provision authorizes magistrates to hold initial appearances at locations other than their offices, such as on location when officers are conducting an impaired driving checkpoint operation with a mobile testing unit (sometimes referred to as a "Batmobile"). Of course, the statute requires magistrates to conduct initial appearances outside of their offices only "to the extent practicable." Some practical issues that might arise include

- lack of access to computer systems and records and
- the ability of the defendant's witnesses to find and gain access to the remote location (the defendant's rights in this regard are discussed below).

In addition, if and when a magistrate decides to conduct initial appearances in a mobile testing unit, the magistrate must remember his or her role as a neutral and independent judicial official[112] and should take steps to dispel any appearance that the magistrate is working with or for the police.

3. Magistrate May Review Alcohol Screening Tests, etc.

When determining whether there is probable cause to believe a person is impaired, a magistrate may review "all alcohol screening tests, chemical analyses, receive testimony from any law enforcement officer concerning impairment and the circumstances of the arrest, and observe the person arrested."[113] Although a positive or negative result on an alcohol screening test can be

---

110. G.S. 20-38.4(a)(1).
111. *Id.*
112. See section I.B.1.
113. G.S. 20-38.4(a)(2).

considered when determining probable cause, the results of the alcohol screening test (e.g., 0.09) cannot be used for that purpose.[114]

4. Impaired Driving Hold Inquiry Is Mandatory

If a magistrate finds probable cause to charge an implied consent offense, the magistrate *must* consider whether an impaired driving hold is required.[115] Before enactment of G.S. 20-38.4(a)(3), some magistrates were not consistently considering impaired driving detentions out of concern about *Knoll* motions, or for other reasons. The statute makes clear that magistrates have no choice but to consider such a detention. The procedure for impaired driving detentions and the *Knoll* case are discussed in section III.F.2.b, below.

5. Special Notifications and Requirements

In implied consent cases, the magistrate must

1. inform the defendant in writing of the established procedure to have people appear at the jail to observe the defendant's condition or to administer an additional chemical analysis if the defendant is unable to make bond and
2. direct a defendant unable to make bond to list everyone he or she wishes to contact, along with their telephone numbers, on a form setting forth the procedure for contacting the persons listed; a copy of the form must be filed with the case file.[116]

Chief district court judges are required to adopt procedures indicating how family, friends, and specified others can gain access to a defendant who has been arrested for an implied consent offense and is unable to obtain pretrial release from jail.[117] Magistrates need to obtain these written procedures so that they can provide the required notice to implied consent offense defendants as required by the statute. The AOC form for certifying compliance with these procedures and on which those people whom the defendant wishes to contact or wants to appear at jail are listed is AOC-CR-271.

---

114. G.S. 20-16.3(d).
115. G.S. 20-38.4(a)(3).
116. G.S. 20-38.4(a)(4).
117. G.S. 20-38.5.

III. Determining the Conditions of Pretrial Release

A. Right to Conditions

1. General Rule: All Defendants Are Entitled to Conditions

Unless the defendant falls within one of the exceptions listed below, the defendant is entitled to have conditions of pretrial release.[118]

2. Exceptions: Defendants Who Are Not Entitled to Conditions from a Magistrate

In certain situations the defendant is not entitled to have conditions set or a magistrate is barred from setting conditions. Table 6 provides an "at-a-glance" listing of these special situations. The sections that follow discuss these situations in more detail.

a. Capital defendants. It is within the discretion of a judge (and only a judge) to decide whether a defendant charged with a capital offense will be released before trial.[119] North Carolina has only one offense that can qualify for capital punishment: first-degree murder.[120] In the unusual situation where a magistrate is faced with setting conditions for a defendant charged with a capital offense, the magistrate should commit the person to jail for a judge to determine the conditions of release at the first appearance.

b. Certain fugitives. A fugitive defendant charged in another state with an offense punishable by death or life imprisonment has no right to pretrial release.[121] Also, a fugitive arrested on a governor's warrant has no right to pretrial release. These defendants should be committed to jail without conditions of release being set. For more information on handling fugitives, see section IV, below.

c. Involuntarily committed defendants who commit crimes while committed. There is no right to pretrial release for a defendant who is alleged to have committed a crime while involuntarily committed or while an escapee from commitment.[122] Such a defendant should be returned to the treatment facility in which he or she was residing at the time of the alleged crime or from which he or she escaped.[123]

d. Certain drug-trafficking offenders. G.S. 15A-533(d) provides that it is presumed (subject to rebuttal by the defendant) that no condition of release will reasonably assure both the appearance of the defendant as required and the safety of the community if a judicial official finds

- reasonable cause to believe that the defendant committed a drug-trafficking offense;
- the drug-trafficking offense was committed while the defendant was on pretrial release for another offense; and

---

118. G.S. 15A-534(b).
119. G.S. 15A-533(c).
120. G.S. 14-7 (first-degree murder may be punished by death or imprisonment for life without parole).
121. G.S. 15A-736.
122. G.S.15A-533(a).
123. *Id.*

Table 6. When Defendant Is Not Entitled to Conditions from a Magistrate

- Capital defendants
- Certain fugitives
- Involuntarily committed defendants who commit crimes while committed
- Certain drug trafficking offenders
- Certain gang crime offenders
- Certain offenses involving firearms
- Violators of health control measures
- Certain methamphetamine offenses
- Military deserters
- Parole violators
- Probation violators with pending felony charge or sex offender status who pose a danger
- Out-of-state probation violators covered by the Interstate Compact
- Defendants subject to a "no release" order issued by a judge

- the defendant has been convicted of a Class A through Class E felony or a drug-trafficking offense and not more than five years have passed since the date of conviction or the defendant's release from prison, whichever is later.

If all of these facts are found, only a district or superior court judge may set pretrial release conditions after finding that there is a reasonable assurance that the defendant will appear and that the release does not pose an unreasonable risk of harm to the community.[124]

e. Certain gang crime offenders. G.S. 15A-533(e) provides that it is presumed (subject to rebuttal by the defendant) that no condition of release will reasonably assure both the appearance of the person as required and the safety of the community if a judicial official finds

- reasonable cause to believe that the person committed an offense for the benefit of, at the direction of, or in association with, any criminal street gang, as defined in G.S. 14-50.16;
- the offense was committed while the person was on pretrial release for another offense; *and*
- the defendant has a previous conviction for a gang offense under G.S. 14-50.16 through -50.20 and not more than five years have passed since the date of conviction or the defendant's release for the offense, whichever is later.

If all of these facts are found, only a district or superior court judge may set pretrial release conditions after finding that there is a reasonable assurance that the defendant will appear and that the release does not pose an unreasonable risk of harm to the community.[125]

f. Certain offenses involving firearms. G.S. 15A-533(f) provides that there is a rebuttable presumption that no condition of release will reasonably assure both the appearance of the person as required and the safety of the community if a judicial official finds

- reasonable cause to believe that the person committed a felony or Class A1 misdemeanor offense involving the illegal use, possession, or discharge of a firearm; *and*

---

124. G.S. 15A-533(g).
125. *Id.*

- the offense was committed while the person was on pretrial release for another felony or Class A1 misdemeanor offense involving the illegal use, possession, or discharge of a firearm; *or*
- the person previously has been convicted of a felony or Class A1 misdemeanor offense involving the illegal use, possession, or discharge of a firearm and not more than five years have elapsed since the date of conviction or the person's release for the offense, whichever is later.

If all of these facts are found, only a district or superior court judge may set pretrial release conditions after finding that there is a reasonable assurance that the defendant will appear and that the release does not pose an unreasonable risk of harm to the community.[126]

g. Violators of health control measures. G.S. 15A-534.5 provides that if a judicial official conducting an initial appearance finds by clear and convincing evidence that a person arrested for violating an order limiting freedom of movement or access issued pursuant to G.S. 130A-475 (incident involving nuclear, biological, or chemical agents) or G.S. 130A-145 (quarantine and isolation authority) poses a threat to the health and safety of others, the judicial official must deny pretrial release. The judicial official must order that the person be confined in a designated area or facility. This pretrial confinement ends when a judicial official determines that the confined person does not pose a threat to the health and safety of others.[127] The statute requires that these determinations be made in conjunction with the recommendation of the state health director or local health director.[128]

h. Certain methamphetamine offenses. G.S. 15A-534.6 authorizes judicial officials to deny pretrial release for specified methamphetamine offenses under certain conditions. The statute provides that a rebuttable presumption arises that no conditions of release would assure the safety of the community if the State shows, by clear and convincing evidence, that

- the defendant was arrested for a violation of G.S. 90-95(b)(1a) (manufacture of methamphetamine) or G.S. 90-95(d1)(2)b (possession of precursor chemical knowing that it will be used to manufacture methamphetamine) *and*
- the defendant is dependent on or has a pattern of regular illegal use of methamphetamine and the violation was committed or attempted to maintain or facilitate the defendant's dependence or use.[129]

i. Military deserters. A military deserter is not entitled to have conditions of pretrial release set by a magistrate.[130] The deserter should be committed to the local detention facility without setting conditions of pretrial release. Military authorities should be contacted as soon as possible to take custody of the deserter.

j. Parole violators. A person taken into custody for a violation of parole or post-release supervision under structured sentencing is not subject to the provisions on pretrial release.[131]

k. Probation violators with pending felony charge or sex offender status who pose a danger. As a general rule, when a defendant has been convicted in North Carolina, put on probation, and later

---

126. *Id.*
127. G.S. 15A-534.5.
128. *Id.*
129. G.S. 15A-534.6.
130. Huff v. Watson, 99 S.E. 307 (Ga. 1919).
131. G.S. 15A-1368.6 (post-release supervision); -1376 (parole).

arrested for a probation violation that occurs in North Carolina, he or she is entitled to conditions of release.[132] However, G.S. 15A-1345(b1) provides that if a probationer is arrested for violating probation and either

- has a pending felony charge *or*
- has been convicted of an offense that requires registration under the sex offender registration statutes or that would have required registration but for the effective date of the registration program,

the judicial official must determine whether the probationer poses a danger to the public before imposing conditions of release and must record that determination in writing. If the judicial official determines that the probationer poses such a danger, the judicial official must deny the probationer release pending the revocation hearing.[133] If the judicial official finds that the defendant does not pose such a danger, the judicial official determines conditions as usual.[134] The procedure for handling the situation where there is insufficient information to make the required determination is discussed in section III.B.2.c.ii, below.

One consequence of this law is that every time a person is brought before a magistrate on an arrest for a probation violation the magistrate will need to know whether the person has a pending felony charge and whether he or she is or could be subject to the sex offender registration program. To determine whether a probation violator has a pending felony charge, the magistrate must do a statewide record search. To determine whether a defendant is subject to the sex offender registration program or could be subject to that program but for its effective date, the magistrate should take the following steps:

1. Search the on-line North Carolina Sex Offender Registry, http://sexoffender.ncdoj.gov, and click on the "Search the Registry" link.[135] If the probation violator's name appears, he or she is subject to G.S. 15A-1345(b1), as discussed above. If the person's name does not appear, go to step 2.
2. Determine the probation violator's prior convictions. If any one of those prior convictions is included in Table 7, the magistrate should apply the provisions of G.S. 15A-1345(b1), as discussed above.

i. Out-of-state probation violators covered by the Interstate Compact. The general rule that probation violators are entitled to conditions of release[136] does not apply to defendants who are arrested on out-of-state warrants for probation violations when the state that imposed the probation and is now seeking to find the defendant in violation of probation has a supervision agreement in place with the State of North Carolina pursuant to the Interstate Compact for Adult Offender Supervision (Interstate Compact).[137] Unlike other out-of-state offenders, out-of-state probation violators covered by Interstate Compact supervision agreements are not dealt with through extradition (see section IV, below); rather, the Interstate Compact statutes govern. One of those statutes, G.S. 148-65.8(a), provides that such a defendant may be detained for up to fifteen days and is not entitled to bail pending the required hearing.

---

132. G.S. 15A-1345(b).
133. G.S. 15A-1345(b1).
134. *Id.*
135. See Figure 3.
136. G.S. 15A-1345(b).
137. G.S. Chapter 148, Article 4B.

Figure 3. Screen Shot of the North Carolina Department of Justice "Search the Registry" Link

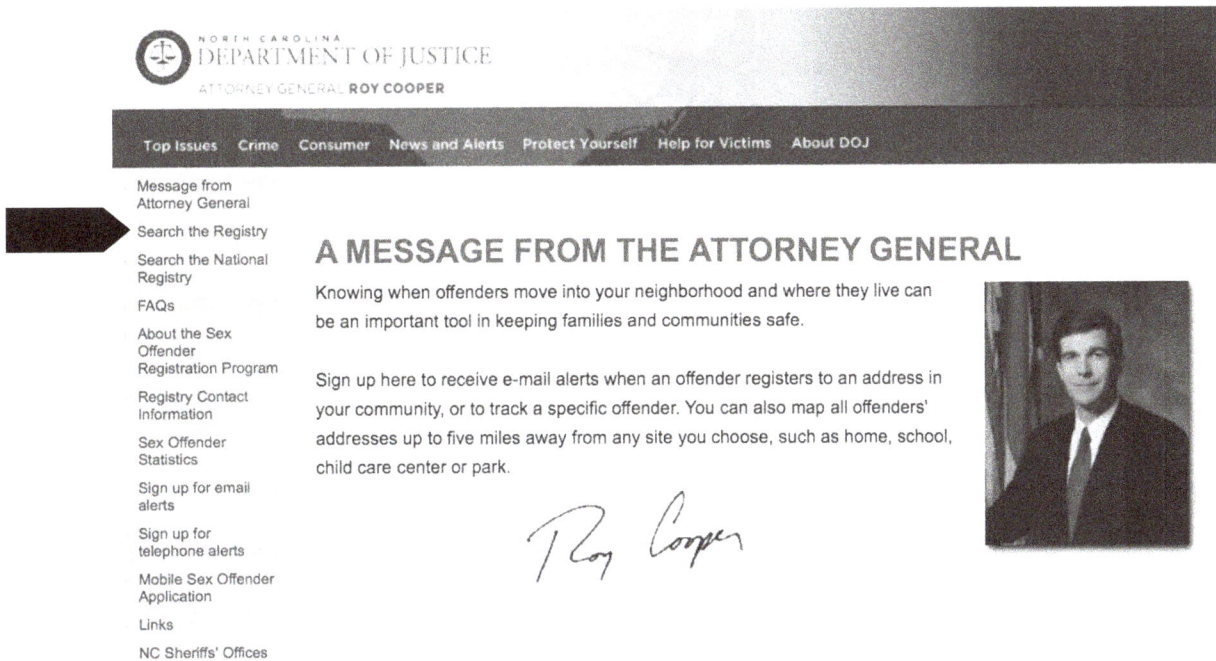

Out-of-state warrants for probation violators covered by the Interstate Compact are supposed to go through the North Carolina compact administrator, a position within the North Carolina Department of Public Safety. If Interstate Compact offenders are processed in this way, the warrant will come to the magistrate with an "Authority to Detain and Hold" form, stating that the offender is not entitled to pretrial release. A sample form is presented as Figure 4. Sometimes, however, the other state fails to go through North Carolina's compact administrator. In such instances it can be difficult for the magistrate to determine whether the person is covered by the Interstate Compact. When this happens, the magistrate can obtain the relevant information from a probation officer. Another alternative is to go to the North Carolina Department of Public Safety webpage, www.doc.state.nc.us, and click on the link "Public Offender Search."[138] From there, enter the offender information, and the search should indicate, below probation and parole status, whether the offender is subject to the Interstate Compact.[139] If so, immediately contact a local probation officer or the North Carolina compact administrator.

> *Practice Pointer*: The North Carolina compact administrator can be reached at (919) 716-3160.

m. Judge's order. The only other situation in which a magistrate can deny a defendant conditions of pretrial release is when expressly ordered to do so by a judge in an order for arrest. Note that a DCI-PIN message that says "no bond" is not a basis for denying pretrial release conditions unless the magistrate can verify that it was ordered by a judge.

---

138. See Figure 5.
139. See Figure 6.

Table 7.   Crimes Requiring Sex Offender Registration (G.S. 14-208.6)

Sexually violent offenses (G.S. 14-208.6(5))
- First-degree rape (G.S. 14-27.2)
- Rape of a child by an adult offender (G.S. 14-27.2A)
- Second-degree rape (G.S. 14-27.3)
- First-degree sexual offense (G.S. 14-27.4)
- Sexual offense with a child by an adult offender (G.S. 14-27.4A)
- Second-degree sexual offense (G.S. 14-27.5)
- Sexual battery (G.S. 14-27.5A)
- Former attempted rape/sexual offense (G.S. 14-27.6)
- Intercourse/sexual offense w/certain victims (G.S. 14-27.7)
- Statutory rape/sexual offense (13–15yo/D 6+ yrs. older) (G.S. 14-27.7A(a))
- Human trafficking (*only if victim < 18 or for sex servitude*) (G.S. 14-43.11)
- Sexual servitude (G.S. 14-43.13)
- Incest between near relatives (G.S. 14-178)
- Employ minor in offense/public morality (G.S. 14-190.6)
- Felony indecent exposure (G.S. 14-190.9(a1))
- First-degree sexual exploitation of minor (G.S. 14-190.16)
- Second-degree sexual exploitation of minor (G.S. 14-190.17)
- Third-degree sexual exploitation of minor (G.S. 14-190.17A)
- Former promoting prostitution of minor (G.S. 14-190.18)
- Former participating in prostitution of minor (G.S. 14-190.19)
- Taking indecent liberties with children (G.S. 14-202.1)
- Solicitation of child by computer (G.S. 14-202.3)
- Taking indecent liberties with a student (G.S. 14-202.4(a))
- Patronizing minor/mentally disabled prostitute (G.S. 14-205.2(c–d))
- Prostitution of minor/mentally disabled child (G.S. 14-205.3(b))
- Parent/caretaker prostitution (G.S. 14-318.4(a1))
- Parent/guardian commit/allow sexual act (G.S. 14-318.4(a2))

Offenses against a minor (G.S. 14-208.6(1m))—Reportable only when victim is a minor and the offender is not the minor's parent.
- Kidnapping (G.S. 14-39)
- Abduction of children (G.S. 14-41)
- Felonious restraint (G.S. 14-43.3)

Peeping crimes (G.S. 14-208.6(4)d.)—Reportable only if the court decides registration furthers purposes of the registry and that the offender is a danger to community.
- Felony peeping under G.S. 14-202 (d), (e), (f), (g), or (h)
- Second/subsequent conviction of:
  misdemeanor peeping under G.S. 14-202(a) or (c) or misdemeanor peeping w/mirror/device under G.S. 14-202(a1)

Sale of a child (G.S. 14-208.6(4)e.)—Reportable only if the sentencing court rules under G.S. 14-43.14(e) that the person is a danger to the community and required to register.

Attempt—Final convictions for attempts to commit an "offense against a minor" or a "sexually violent offense" are reportable. G.S. 14-208.6(4)a.

Conspiracy/Solicitation—Conspiracy and solicitation to commit an "offense against a minor" or a "sexually violent offense" are reportable. G.S. 14-208.6(1m); -208.6(5).

Aiding and Abetting—Aiding and abetting an "offense against a minor" or "sexually violent offense" is reportable *only* if the court finds that registration furthers the purposes of the registry (set out in G.S. 14-208.5). G.S. 14-208.6(4)a.

Figure 4.   Sample Authority to Detain and Hold Form

North Carolina Department of Public Safety

Community Supervision – North Carolina Interstate Compact

Pat McCrory, Governor
Frank L. Perry, Secretary

W. David Guice, Commissioner
Anne L. Precythe, Director

AUTHORITY TO DETAIN AND HOLD

TO ANY OFFICER AUTHORIZED BY LAW TO DETAIN AND HOLD:

_____ is an out-of-state offender from the State of _____,
          (Name)   (State)
who is presently being supervised by the North Carolina Department of Public Safety, Community Supervision.

        Based on facts presented to this Office, there is probable cause to believe that said out-of-state offender has violated the terms or conditions of supervision and must therefore be detained and held pending a probable cause hearing on the issue.

Pursuant to section 148-65.8 of the General Statutes of North Carolina and the rules of the Interstate Compact Agreement for the Supervision of Adult Offenders granted by Congress, (48 Stat.909, 4 U.S.C. Section 112), you are hereby authorized and directed to detain and hold:

_____
                        (Name)

_____
                        (Address)

The out-of-state offender is to be held at any suitable institution other than a North Carolina Adult Correction Prison Facility.

ATTENTION MAGISTRATE: THIS OUT-OF-STATE OFFENDER IS NOT SUBJECT TO BOND.

A probable cause hearing will be held within 15 days from the date placed in custody unless such hearing is waived by the offender. Upon conclusion of the probable cause hearing, the offender is not entitled to any judicial proceedings in North Carolina in this matter. All legal requirements to obtain extradition of fugitives from justice are expressly waived.

Immediately call this Office at (919) 716-3160 when said offender is taken into custody.

This the _____day of_____, 20_____.

_____
Jay Lynn, Deputy Compact Administrator
NC Department of Public Safety, Community Supervision
Office: 919-716-3160
Fax: 919-716-3999

NOTICE
DO NOT RELEASE THIS OFFENDER BEFORE CONTACTING THE DEPUTY COMPACT ADMINISTRATOR

**Attachments: Out of State Warrant/Violation Report
                Application for Offender Transfer**

MAILING ADDRESS:
4259 Mail Service Center
Raleigh, NC 27699-4259
Telephone: (919) 716-3160

OFFICE LOCATION:
2020 Yonkers Road
Raleigh, NC 27604
Fax: (919) 716-3999

www.ncdps.gov
An Equal Opportunity employer

Figure 5.   North Carolina Department of Public Safety Page Link to a Public Offender Search

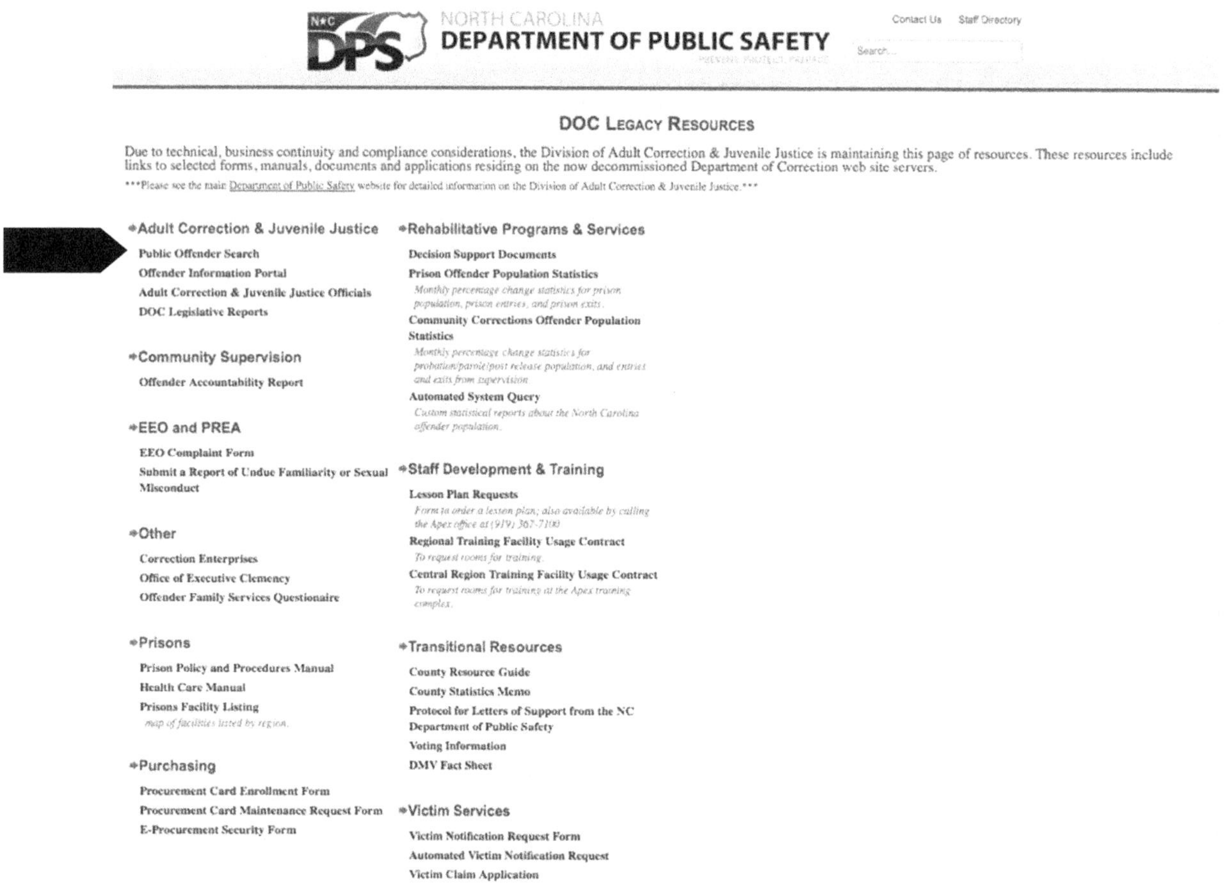

Figure 6.   Redacted Sample Results from Public Offender Search

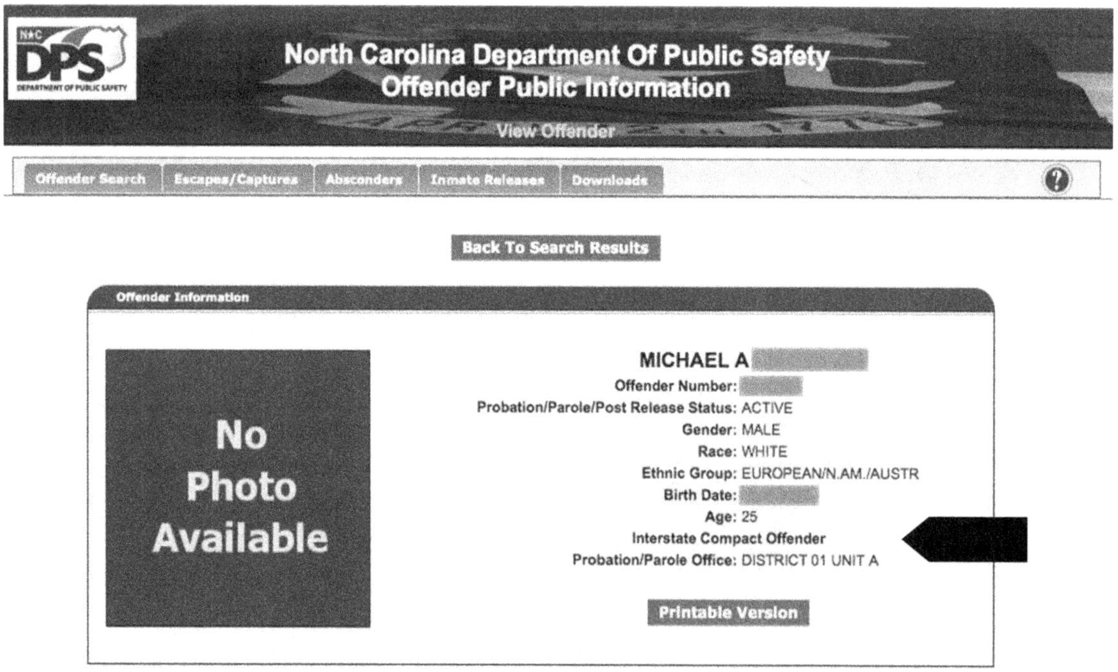

B. Time for Determining Conditions

1. General Rule: At Initial Appearance

Normally, the time for determining conditions is at the initial appearance.[140]

2. Exceptions: Delaying the Setting of Conditions

In certain situations, the law requires a delay in the setting of conditions. Those situations are discussed in the subsections that follow. Note that a prior section discussed when a magistrate may delay the initial appearance altogether,[141] and a later one discusses when a defendant's release may be delayed, even if he or she has satisfied the conditions of pretrial release.[142]

a. Forty-eight-hour rule for domestic violence cases. Whenever a defendant is charged with

- an assault on, stalking, communicating a threat to, or committing a felony as provided in G.S. Chapter 14, Articles 7A, 8, 10, or 15, upon a current or former spouse or a person with whom the defendant lives or has lived as if married,
- domestic criminal trespass, *or*
- a violation of a 50B order,

only a judge can set conditions of pretrial release in the forty-eight-hour period after an arrest.[143] Thus, when a defendant is brought before a magistrate for an offense covered by this provision, the magistrate should hold an initial appearance and order the defendant held for the next available session of district or superior court to have conditions of release determined by a judge.

> *Practice Pointer*: To do this in NCAWARE or on the release order form, AOC-CR-200, check the box in the "Order of Commitment" portion that states "Check in all domestic violence cases covered by G.S. 15A-534.1(b)." Then enter an appropriate date and time as instructed.

If a judge does not act within forty-eight hours, the magistrate sets conditions.[144] Note that if forty-eight hours expire and the defendant is brought before a magistrate, the magistrate must "direct a law enforcement officer or a district attorney to provide a criminal history report for the defendant and shall consider the criminal history when setting conditions of release."[145] After setting conditions of release, the magistrate must return the report to the providing agency or department.[146] Also, a magistrate may not unreasonably delay the determination of conditions of pretrial release so that he or she can review the defendant's criminal history report.[147]

A helpful chart listing common offenses covered by the forty-eight-hour rule is posted on the SOG's web page for magistrates, www.sog.unc.edu/node/140. From that site, click on the link "Domestic Violence: 48-Hour Rule Offense Chart."[148]

---

140. See section II.A, above.
141. See section II.B.2, above.
142. See section III.F.2, below.
143. G.S. 15A-534.1.
144. G.S. 15A-534.1(b).
145. G.S. 15A-534.1(a).
146. *Id.*
147. *Id.*
148. See Figure 7.

Figure 7.   Screen Shot of North Carolina Magistrates' Web Page, Showing Link to the 48-Hour Rule Offense Chart

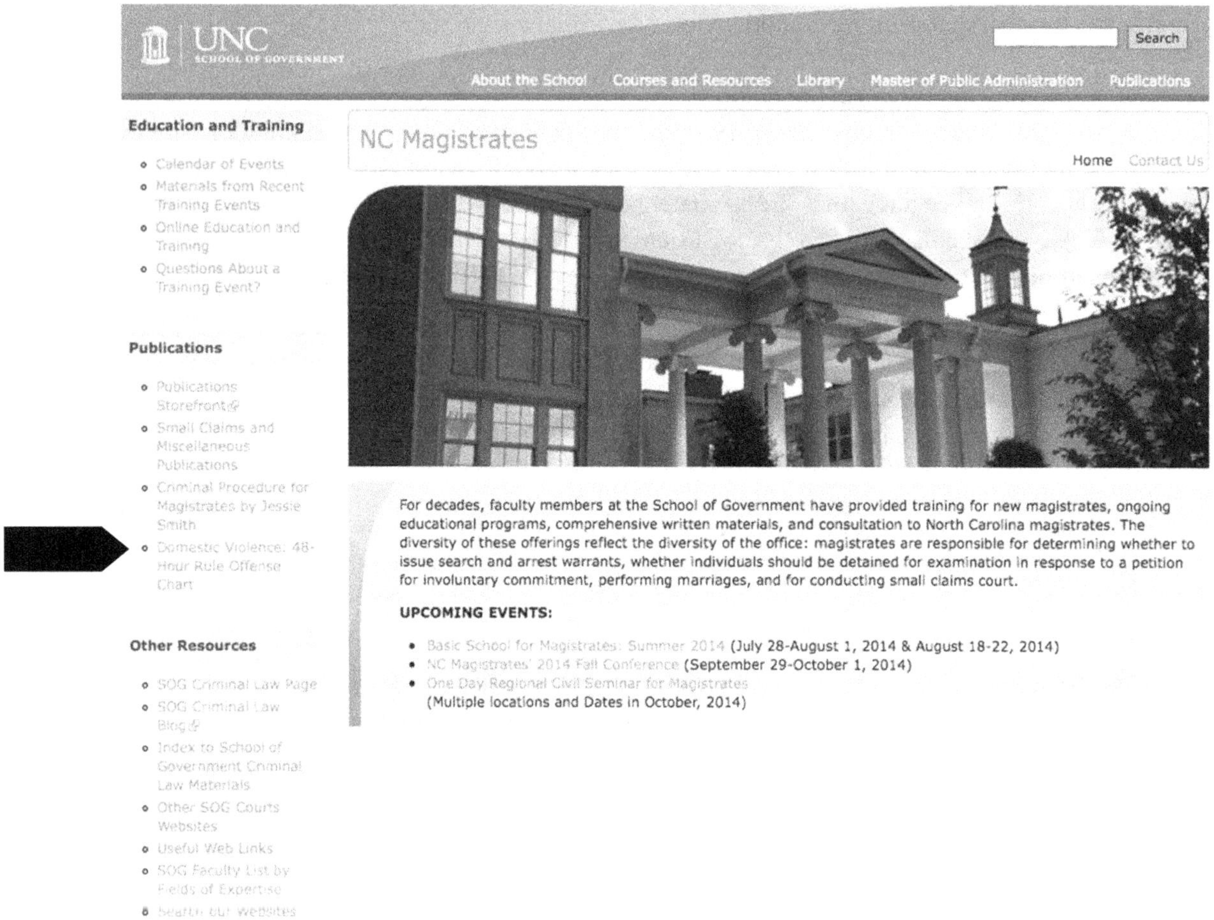

b. Other domestic violence holds. G.S. 15A-534.1(a)(1) provides another domestic violence hold for defendants who are charged with an assault on, stalking, communicating a threat to, or committing a felony as provided in G.S. Chapter 14, Articles 7A, 8, 10, or 15, upon a current or former spouse or a person with whom the defendant lives or has lived as if married, with domestic criminal trespass or with a violation of a 50B order. The statute provides that upon a determination that the defendant's immediate release will pose a danger of injury to the alleged victim or another person or is likely to result in intimidation of the alleged victim and upon a determination that the execution of an appearance bond will not reasonably assure that such injury will not occur, a judicial official may retain the defendant in custody for a reasonable period of time while determining conditions of pretrial release.[149] It is unlikely that a magistrate will have an opportunity to apply this provision. Only a judge can set conditions of pretrial release within the first forty-eight hours of the defendant's arrest (see the section immediately above); once forty-eight hours have expired, it is unlikely that the circumstances would warrant application of this exception.

---

149. G.S. 15A-534.1(a)(1).

c. Probation cases

i. Defendant charged with felony while on probation and magistrate cannot assess danger

When conditions of pretrial release are being determined for a defendant who is charged with a felony while on probation for an earlier offense, a magistrate must determine whether the defendant poses a danger to the public (and make a written record of that determination) before imposing conditions of pretrial release.[150] If the defendant does not pose such a danger, he or she is entitled to release as in any other case.[151] If the defendant poses such a danger, the magistrate must impose a secured bond or a secured bond with electronic house arrest.[152] However, if there is insufficient information to determine whether the defendant poses a danger, the magistrate must keep the defendant in custody until that determination can be made.[153] If a magistrate detains the defendant for this reason, the magistrate must make a written record, at the time of the detention, of the following:

1. the fact that the defendant is being held pursuant to G.S. 15A-534(d2);
2. the basis for the decision that additional information is needed to determine whether the defendant poses a danger to the public and the nature of the necessary information; and
3. a date, within ninety-six hours of the time of arrest, when the defendant will be brought before a judge for a first appearance.[154]

If the necessary information is provided to the court at any time before the first appearance, the first available judicial official must set the conditions of pretrial release.[155]

One consequence of this statute is that every time a defendant is brought before a magistrate on a felony charge, the magistrate must determine whether the defendant is on probation for an earlier offense. If so, the new statutory procedure must be followed. Form AOC-CR-272 is designed to be used in these cases.

ii. Probation violator who has pending felony or is sex offender and magistrate cannot assess danger

If a probationer is arrested for violating probation and either

- has a pending felony charge *or*
- has been convicted of an offense that requires registration under the sex offender registration statutes or that would have required registration but for the effective date of the registration program,

the magistrate must determine whether the probationer poses a danger to the public (and make a written record of that determination) before imposing conditions of release.[156] If the probationer does not pose such a danger, the magistrate should determine the conditions of release as in any other case.[157] If the probationer poses such a danger, he or she must be denied release.[158] If there is insufficient information to determine whether the defendant poses such a danger, the magistrate

---

150. G.S. 15A-534(d2).
151. *Id.*
152. *Id.*
153. *Id.*
154. *Id.*
155. *Id.*
156. G.S. 15A-1345(b1).
157. *Id.*
158. *Id.*

must detain the defendant in custody for no more than seven days from the date of the arrest to obtain sufficient information to make that determination.[159] If the defendant has been held seven days from the date of arrest and the court has been unable to obtain sufficient information to determine whether the defendant poses a danger to the public, the defendant must then be brought before any judicial official, who must record that fact in writing and must impose conditions of pretrial release.[160]

One consequence of this statute is that every time a person is brought before a magistrate for a probation violation, the magistrate will need to determine whether he or she has a pending felony charge and whether he or she is or could be subject to the sex offender registration program. If so, the new statutory procedure must be followed. Form AOC-CR-272 is designed to be used in such cases. For a discussion of how to determine whether a probationer has a pending felony charge or is or could be subject to the sex offender registration program, see section III.A.2.k, above.

C. Selecting Pretrial Release Conditions

1. Five Core Options

G.S. 15A-534(a) provides that when determining conditions of pretrial release, a judicial official must impose at least one of the five conditions shown in the sidebar on page 39.

a. Written promise to appear. This release involves no money. The defendant simply is released on his or her written promise to appear in court.[161]

b. Custody release. A custody release is a release to a designated person or organization that agrees to supervise the defendant.[162] Like a release on a written promise to appear, no money is involved. If this condition is imposed, the defendant may elect instead to execute a secured appearance bond.[163] Note that a custody release is not the same as a release to a sober responsible adult in connection with an impaired driving hold.[164]

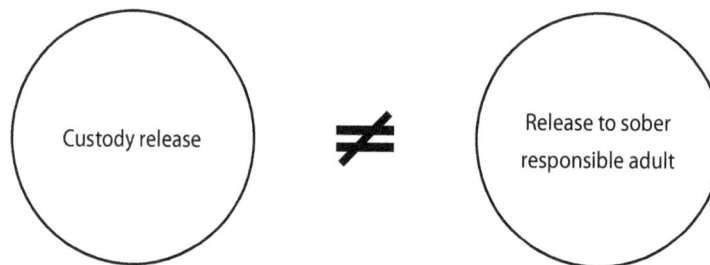

c. Unsecured bond. An unsecured bond is a bond backed only by the integrity of the defendant, not by assets or collateral.[165]

---

159. *Id.*
160. *Id.*
161. *See generally* G.S. 15A-534(a)(1).
162. G.S.15A-534(a)(3).
163. G.S. 15A-534(a).
164. See section III.F.2.b (discussing impaired driving holds).
165. *See generally* G.S. 15A-534(a)(2).

```
┌─────────────────────────────────────────────────┐
│              Pretrial Release Options             │
│              ─────────────────────                │
│                                                   │
│   • Written promise to appear                     │
│   • Custody release                               │
│   • Unsecured bond                                │
│   • Secured bond                                  │
│   • House arrest with electronic monitoring       │
│                                                   │
└─────────────────────────────────────────────────┘
```

d. Secured bond. A secured appearance bond is a bond backed by a cash deposit in the full amount of the bond, by a mortgage, or by at least one solvent surety.[166]

G.S. 15A-534 suggests that when a magistrate designates a secured bond as the condition of release, the magistrate may not also dictate which type of secured bond a defendant may post. Therefore, even if a magistrate sees that a judge has set a cash bond or a "green money only" bond on one or more occasions, the magistrate should not assume that he or she has authority to specify a cash bond. On this issue magistrates should consult the written bond policy issued by the senior resident superior court judge. If the written policy does not address this issue, magistrates should seek advice from the senior resident superior court judge or chief district court judge before setting a cash bond.

e. House arrest with electronic monitoring. If this condition is imposed, the magistrate also must impose a secured appearance bond.[167] This condition is relatively new, and it is not yet clear how this condition will be implemented or which jurisdictions are equipped to implement it. Because imposing this condition in the absence of available equipment will result in a hold, if the county lacks the available equipment or does not have a device immediately available for the defendant involved, the magistrate should check with his or her supervising judge before imposing this condition.

2. Release to Pretrial Release Program

In counties that have pretrial release programs, the senior resident superior court judge may order that defendants who both consent to be released to the program and are accepted into the program be released to the program when a written promise, unsecured bond, or custody release has been ordered.[168]

3. What to Consider When Setting Conditions

a. Local procedure. When setting conditions of pretrial release, magistrates should follow the written pretrial release policy issued by the senior resident superior court judge. Note that G.S. 15A-535 provides that the senior resident superior court judge must create and issue recommended pretrial release policies. Magistrates should obtain a copy of their written local procedures.

---

166. G.S. 15A-534(a)(4).
167. G.S. 15A-534(a).
168. G.S. 15A-535(b).

b. Purpose of conditions of pretrial release. The purpose of conditions of pretrial release is to make sure that the defendant appears in court when required and does no harm while on release. Magistrates should keep these purposes in mind when deciding which conditions to impose.

c. Relevant factors. The statutory scheme expresses a preference for written promises, unsecured bonds, and custody releases. In fact, the statute states that a judicial official must impose these conditions unless the official determines that such a release "will not reasonably assure the appearance of the defendant as required; will pose a danger of injury to any person; or is likely to result in destruction of evidence, subornation of perjury, or intimidation of potential witnesses."[169] If the judicial official so finds, he or she must impose a secured bond or house arrest with electronic monitoring (and secured bond) and record the reason for doing so if required by local policy.[170] G.S. 15A-534(c) provides that in determining which conditions of release to impose, a magistrate must, on the basis of available information, take into account

- the nature and circumstances of the offense charged;
- the weight of the evidence against the defendant;
- the defendant's family ties, employment, financial resources, character, and mental condition;
- whether the defendant is intoxicated to such a degree that he or she would be endangered by being released without supervision;
- the length of the defendant's residence in the community;
- the defendant's record of convictions;
- the defendant's history of flight to avoid prosecution or failure to appear at court proceedings; and
- any other evidence relevant to the issue of pretrial release.

For defendants charged with violating G.S. 90-95(b)(la) (manufacture of methamphetamine) or G.S. 90-95(dl)(2)b (possession of precursor chemical knowing that it will be used to manufacture methamphetamine), the magistrate must also consider any evidence that the person "is in any manner dependent upon methamphetamine or has a pattern of regular illegal use of methamphetamine."[171]

d. Relevant evidence. G.S. 15A-534(g) provides that when imposing conditions of pretrial release a magistrate must take into account all available evidence that he or she considers reliable. The magistrate is not bound by the rules of evidence when making this determination.[172]

4. When the Magistrate's Discretion Is Limited

As a general rule, and subject to local bond policy, the law gives magistrates a great deal of discretion to determine the appropriate conditions of pretrial release. In some situations, however, the law or a judge requires a magistrate to impose certain conditions, forbids the magistrate from imposing certain conditions, or allows the magistrate to consider special conditions. This section discusses those special situations.

a. Infractions. As a general rule any person who is not a North Carolina resident and is charged with an infraction may be required to post a bond to secure his or her appearance in court.[173] The charging officer may require the person to accompany the officer to the magistrate's office

---

169. G.S. 15A-534(b).
170. *Id.*
171. G.S. 15A-534.6.
172. G.S. 15A-534(g).
173. G.S. 15A-1113(c).

Figure 8. Conditions for Probationers Charged with a Felony

Does Probationer Charged with a Felony Pose a Danger to the Public?

Yes	No	Can't Determine
Impose secured bond or EHA with secured bond	Set conditions as usual	Detain as discussed in section III.B.2.c.i

to determine if a bond is necessary to secure the person's court appearance and, if so, what kind of bond is to be used.[174] However, if a magistrate finds that the person is unable to post a secured bond, the magistrate *must* allow the person to be released by executing an unsecured bond.[175]

There are three exceptions to this rule:

1. A North Carolina resident who is charged with an infraction cannot be required to post bond.[176]
2. A person charged with an infraction cannot be required to post an appearance bond if the person is licensed to drive by a state that is a member of the motor vehicle nonresident violator compact, the charged infraction is subject to the compact, and the person executes a personal recognizance required by the compact.[177]
3. Certain individuals charged with infractions that are subject to the Wildlife Violator Compact cannot be required to post a bond.[178]

b. Probationer charged with a felony. When determining conditions of pretrial release for a defendant who is charged with a felony while he or she was on probation for an earlier offense, the magistrate must determine whether the defendant poses a danger to the public before imposing conditions of pretrial release and must record that determination in writing.[179] If the magistrate determines that the defendant poses a danger to the public, the magistrate must impose a secured bond or electronic house arrest (with secured bond).[180] If the magistrate finds that the defendant does not pose a danger to the public, the magistrate should impose conditions as usual.[181] When the information is insufficient to make the required determination, the magistrate must detain the defendant in custody until a determination of pretrial release conditions can be made.[182] (See Figure 8.)

c. Prior failures to appear and bond doubling. When conditions of pretrial release are being imposed on a defendant who has failed to appear for the charges to which the conditions apply, the judicial official must, at a minimum, impose the conditions recommended by the OFA.[183] If no conditions are recommended in the OFA, the judicial official must require a secured bond that is at least

---

174. *Id.*
175. *Id.*
176. G.S. 15A-1113(c)(2).
177. G.S. 15A-1113(c)(1).
178. G.S. 113-300.6.
179. G.S. 15A-534(d2).
180. G.S. 15A-534(d2)(1).
181. G.S. 15A-534(d2)(2).
182. See section III.B.2.c.i, above.
183. G.S. 15A-534(d1).

Failure to Appear and Bond Doubling—Examples

Example 1: Defendant is brought to the magistrate on an OFA after a failure to appear. In the OFA, the judge specified a $5,000 secured bond. The magistrate should impose a $5,000 secured bond.

Example 2: Defendant is brought to the magistrate on an OFA after a failure to appear. The judge's OFA is silent on conditions. The prior bond on the charges is $1,000 unsecured. The magistrate must impose a bond of at least double the bond and make it secured.

Example 3: Defendant is brought to the magistrate on an OFA after a failure to appear. The judge's OFA is silent on conditions. The defendant had previously been released on a custody release. The magistrate must impose a secured bond of at least $1,000 secured.

---

double the amount of the most recent previous bond (secured or unsecured) for the charges or, if no bond has yet been set, a secured bond of at least $1,000.[184] In these situations, the judicial official also must impose such restrictions on the defendant's travel, associations, conduct, or place of abode to assure that the defendant will not again fail to appear.[185] In addition, the judicial official must indicate on the release order that the defendant was arrested or surrendered after failing to appear as required under a prior release order.[186] If available information indicates that the defendant has failed on two or more prior occasions to appear to answer the charges, the magistrate must note that on the release order.[187]

> *Practice Pointers*: If the defendant has been arrested on an OFA after a failure to appear (FTA), it is best to check for a prior surrender by the surety for the same failure to appear. If that has happened and a new release order has been entered and a new bond set, re-release the defendant on the bond already posted and attempt to have the OFA recalled. If the defendant has not already been surrendered by a surety for the same FTA, set conditions of release as described above.
>
> If the defendant has been surrendered by a surety after an FTA, it is best to check to see whether the defendant already has been arrested by a law enforcement officer for the same FTA. If so, and a new release order has been entered and new bond posted, re-release the defendant on the bond already posted. If the defendant has not already been arrested, try to recall any outstanding OFA so that the defendant will not be re-arrested for the same FTA. Then, set conditions of release as described above.

d. Defendants already on pretrial release and bond doubling. When conditions of pretrial release are being determined for a defendant who is charged with an offense and the defendant is currently on pretrial release for a prior offense, the judicial official must require the execution of a secured bond of at least double the amount of the most recent previous bond (secured or unsecured) for the charges or, if no bond has yet been required for the charges, in the amount of at least $1,000.[188]

---

184. *Id.*

185. *Id.*

186. *Id.*

187. *Id.*

188. G.S. 15A-534(d3). For a discussion of some issues related to this new provision, see Jeff Welty, *Double Bond*, North Carolina Criminal Law blog (Mar. 19, 2014), http://nccriminallaw.sog.unc.edu/?p=4676.

Pretrial Release Offenders and Bond Doubling—Examples

Example 1: Defendant is brought to the magistrate on DWI charges. Defendant is currently on pretrial release for an assault charge. The pretrial release conditions for the assault charge include a $500 unsecured bond. The magistrate must impose a secured bond of at least double that amount.

Example 2: Defendant is brought to the magistrate on DWI charges. Defendant is currently on pretrial release for an assault charge. The defendant was released on personal recognizance on the assault charge. The magistrate must impose a secured bond of at least $1,000.

---

e. Order of a judge. If the judge has ordered that certain conditions of pretrial release be imposed—for example, in an OFA—the magistrate should impose those conditions as ordered.

D. Other Conditions

In addition to the pretrial release options discussed above, other restrictions and conditions are permitted and, in some cases, required.

1. Restrictions on Travel, Association, etc.

G.S. 15A-534(a) authorizes magistrates to impose restrictions on travel, associations, conduct, or place of abode. Magistrates are allowed to impose these restrictions no matter what type of pretrial release condition they set. Any restrictions imposed should be reasonable and related to the purpose of pretrial release. Restrictions should not be used as punishment.

2. Domestic Violence Cases

Special restrictions may be imposed on a defendant who is charged with

- an assault on, stalking, communicating a threat to, or committing a felony as provided in G.S. Chapter 14, Articles 7A, 8, 10, or 15, upon a current or former spouse or a person with whom the defendant lives or has lived as if married,
- domestic criminal trespass, *or*
- a violation of a 50B order.[189]

These offenses are often referred to as forty-eight-hour rule offenses. A helpful chart listing common offenses covered by the forty-eight-hour rule is posted on the SOG's web page for magistrates, www.sog.unc.edu/node/140. At that site, click on the link "Domestic Violence: 48-Hour Rule Offense Chart."[190]

Those restrictions include that the defendant

- stay away from the home, school, business, or place of employment of the alleged victim;
- refrain from assaulting, beating, molesting, or wounding the alleged victim;
- refrain from removing, damaging, or injuring specifically identified property;
- may visit his or her child or children at times and places provided by the terms of any existing order entered by a judge;

---

189. G.S. 15A-534.1 (a).
190. See Figure 7.

- abstain from alcohol consumption, as verified by the use of a continuous alcohol monitoring system of a type approved by the Division of Adult Correction of the Department of Public Safety, and that any violation of this condition be reported by the monitoring provider to the district attorney.[191]

Form AOC-CR-630 is designed to be used for this purpose.

3. Certain Cases Involving Child Victims

Under G.S. 15A-534.3, specific conditions must be imposed on a defendant who is charged with certain sex offenses or crimes of violence against child victims listed in Table 8.[192] If the defendant is charged with one of those crimes, the magistrate must impose conditions that the defendant

1. stay away from the victim's home, temporary residence, school, business, or place of employment;
2. refrain from communicating or attempting to communicate with the victim, except as specified in an order entered by a judge with knowledge of the pending charges; and
3. refrain from assaulting, beating, intimidating, stalking, threatening, or harming the alleged victim.[193]

However, upon request of the defendant, the magistrate may waive one or both of conditions (1) and (2) if the magistrate makes written findings of fact that it is not in the best interest of the alleged victim that the condition or conditions be imposed.[194] Form AOC-CR-631 is designed for these cases.

4. Prior Failures to Appear and Bond Doubling

As noted in section III.C.4.c, above, when conditions of pretrial release are being imposed on a defendant who has failed to appear for the charges to which the conditions apply, the judicial official also must impose such restrictions on the defendant's travel, associations, conduct, or place of abode to assure that the defendant will not again fail to appear.[195]

5. Fingerprints and DNA Samples

If the defendant is required to provide fingerprints pursuant to G.S. 15A-502(a1) or (a2), or a DNA sample pursuant to G.S. 15A-266.3A or G.S. 15A-266.4, and

- the fingerprints or DNA sample have not yet been taken *or*
- the defendant has refused to provide the fingerprints or DNA sample,

the judicial official must make the collection of the fingerprints or DNA sample a condition of pretrial release.[196]

---

191. G.S. 15A-534.1(a)(2).
192. G.S. 15A-534.4.
193. *Id.*
194. *Id.*
195. G.S. 15A-534(d1).
196. G.S. 15A-534(a).

Table 8. Child Abuse Crimes Triggering G.S. 15A-534.4

- Felonious or misdemeanor child abuse
- Taking indecent liberties with a minor in violation of G.S. 14-202.1
- Rape or any other sex offense in violation of G.S. Chapter 14, Article 7A against a minor victim
- Incest with a minor in violation of G.S. 14-178
- Kidnapping, abduction, or felonious restraint involving a minor
- Transporting a child outside the state with intent to violate a custody order, as prohibited by G.S. 14-320.1
- Assault or any other crime of violence against a minor
- Communicating a threat against a minor

6. Continuous Alcohol Monitoring

The judicial official may include as a condition of pretrial release that the defendant abstain from alcohol consumption, as verified by the use of a continuous alcohol monitoring system of a type approved by the Division of Adult Correction of the Department of Public Safety, and that any violation of this condition be reported by the monitoring provider to the district attorney.[197]

E. The Pretrial Release Order

The judicial official authorizing pretrial release must issue an order stating the conditions imposed.[198] The official also must inform the defendant in writing of the penalties that will apply to violations of release conditions and advise the defendant that his or her arrest will be ordered immediately upon any violation.[199] The order must be filed with the clerk, and a copy must be given to the defendant.[200] Form AOC-CR-200 is designed for this purpose. The NCAWARE system is designed to track the form.

F. Releasing a Defendant

1. Generally

Subject to the exceptions noted below, a defendant must be released when he or she has satisfied the conditions of release.[201] A written promise to appear or a custody release is satisfied by having the defendant and the custodian sign the appropriate sections of the Conditions of Release and Release Order form (AOC-CR-200). However, when a bond is set—whether secured or unsecured—an appearance bond is required. In addition, as noted above, imposition of electronic monitoring as a condition also requires a secured bond. The procedures for taking an appearance bond are detailed and technical. They are not covered here but are fully addressed by AOC legal staff in the memorandum that appears in the appendix to this publication. Form AOC-CR-201 is the appearance bond form.

---

197. G.S. 15A-534(a).
198. G.S. 15A-534(d).
199. *Id.*
200. *Id.*
201. G.S. 15A-537(a).

2. Exceptions: When Release Is Delayed

As noted above, the general procedure for initial appearances is to conduct the initial appearance without delay, make a probable cause determination and if probable cause is found, inform the defendant of his or her rights, and set conditions of pretrial release. Sections above discuss several exceptions to this general rule.[202] This section discusses another exception: when the magistrate holds the initial appearance, sets conditions of pretrial release, but delays the defendant's release. Only two situations fall within this exception; both are discussed below.

a. Communicable disease holds. Under G.S. 15A-534.3, if a magistrate finds probable cause to believe that a person was exposed to the defendant in a manner that poses a significant risk, through nonsexual contact, of transmission of the AIDS virus or Hepatitis B infection, the magistrate must order the defendant detained for a reasonable period, not to exceed twenty-four hours, for investigation by public health officials and testing, if required by those officials under G.S. 130A-144 and -148. AOC-CR-270, side two, is used for this purpose.

Note that magistrates can contact a public health official for advice on whether the person was in fact exposed to the defendant in a manner posing a significant risk of transmission when deciding whether probable cause exists to justify detaining the defendant.

> *Practice Pointer*: Contact information for all county health departments in North Carolina is available at www.ncalhd.org/county.htm.

Although G.S. 15A-534.3 does not address whether the magistrate should set pretrial release conditions that would be applicable after the defendant has been examined by public health officials, it probably would be wise to do so. That way, once the public health officials have completed their investigation and testing, the defendant will not have to be brought back again before a magistrate for the setting of pretrial release conditions.

b. Impaired driving holds. Impaired driving detentions under G.S. 15A-534.2 cause more confusion among magistrates than almost any other area of criminal procedure. This section breaks down the statute's requirements.

i. "Triggering" offenses

G.S. 15A-534.2 contains a special detention provision that applies when a magistrate finds probable cause to charge the defendant with one or more of the offenses listed in Table 9.

ii. Relevant determination

An impaired driving detention must be imposed when a magistrate finds both probable cause to charge the defendant with one of the offenses listed in Table 9 and clear and convincing evidence that if the defendant is released his or her physical or mental impairment presents a danger of physical injury to himself or herself or others or of damage to property.[203] The determination under G.S. 15A-534.2 is not optional. G.S. 20-38.4 makes it clear that once there is a finding of probable cause that the defendant committed a "triggering" offense a magistrate must determine whether an impaired driving detention must be imposed. Before enactment of G.S. 20-38.4, some magistrates reported that impaired driving detentions were not done in their counties out of concern that the underlying criminal case would have to be dismissed on a "*Knoll* motion." This concern

---

202. See section II.B.2 (discussing when the initial appearance may be delayed) and section III.B.2 (discussing when a magistrate may delay setting conditions).

203. G.S. 15A-534.2(b).

Table 9. Offenses That Can Trigger an Impaired Driving Hold

- Impaired driving under G.S. 20-138.1
- Impaired driving in a commercial vehicle under G.S. 20-138.2
- Habitual impaired driving under G.S. 20-138.5
- Any death by vehicle or serious injury by vehicle offense under G.S. 20-141.4, when based on impaired driving or a substantially similar offense under previous law
- First- or second-degree murder under G.S. 14-17 or involuntary manslaughter under G.S. 14-18, when based on impaired driving

stemmed from a belief that the North Carolina Supreme Court's decision in *State v. Knoll*[204] invalidates a magistrate's authority to order a detention of impaired drivers under G.S. 15A-534.2. This suggestion, however, is incorrect. *Knoll* involved situations where magistrates failed to follow statutory procedures, including failing to advise defendants of their rights and declining to release them to appropriate adults. Cases since *Knoll* suggest that if a magistrate complies with G.S. 15A-534.2, no *Knoll* violation will be found. In any event, G.S. 20-38.4 now makes it clear that magistrates are required to make the impaired driving detention determination.

iii. Detention ordered

If the magistrate finds probable cause that the defendant committed one of the offenses in Table 9 and clear and convincing evidence that the defendant's impairment presents a danger as described above, the magistrate must order the defendant detained until one of the following events occurs:

- the defendant's impairment no longer presents a danger of physical injury to himself or herself or others or of damage to property *or*
- a sober, responsible adult (eighteen years of age or older) is willing and able to assume responsibility for the defendant until the defendant's physical and mental faculties are no longer impaired.[205]

iv. Notification of rights and listing of persons to contact

As discussed in section II.J.5, above, in implied consent cases (this category of cases includes offenses involving impaired driving subject to G.S. 15A-534.2 as well as other offenses), G.S. 20-38.4 requires a magistrate to

1. inform the person in writing of the established procedure to have others appear at the jail to observe the person's condition or to administer an additional chemical analysis if the person is unable to make bond and
2. require anyone unable to make bond to list everyone he or she wishes to contact, along with their telephone numbers, on a form setting forth the procedure for contacting the persons listed; a copy of that form must be filed with the case file.[206]

Also as noted in section II.J.5, above, each chief district court judge must adopt procedures indicating how family, friends, and specified others can gain access to a defendant who has been

---

204. 322 N.C. 535 (1988).
205. G.S. 15A-534.2(c).
206. G.S. 20-38.4(a)(4).

arrested for an implied consent offense and is unable to obtain pretrial release from jail. Magistrates need to obtain these written procedures so that they can provide the required notice to defendants as required by the statute. The form used for these purposes is AOC-CR-271.

v. Effect of the detention

Once the defendant meets one of the two conditions above (impairment no longer a danger or release to sober, responsible adult), the defendant still must satisfy the conditions of pretrial release (for example, $500 secured bond) before he or she can be released.[207]

vi. Written findings required

Whenever a magistrate orders a defendant detained under G.S. 15A-534.2, the magistrate must make written findings to support the detention.[208] Form AOC-CR-270, side one, should be used for this purpose.

vii. Timing of the detention decision

A magistrate should decide at the time of the initial appearance whether or not to detain the defendant under G.S. 15A-534.2. If a defendant is detained under G.S. 15A-534.2, the magistrate still must determine the conditions of pretrial release.[209]

viii. Maximum period of the detention

A defendant may not be detained under G.S. 15A-534.2 for longer than twenty-four hours, even if he or she never meets one of the two conditions. However, at the end of the twenty-four-hour period, the defendant still must satisfy the conditions of pretrial release before being released.[210]

When making the determination of whether or not a detained defendant remains impaired, the magistrate may request that the defendant take periodic tests to determine his or her alcohol concentration.[211] The testing instrument may be an instrument acceptable for making preliminary breath tests under G.S. 20-16.3 (commonly referred to as a mobile testing unit) or evidentiary chemical analysis (currently the Intoximeter, Model Intox EC/IR II).[212] If the defendant takes a test and the results indicate that his or her alcohol concentration is less than 0.05, the magistrate must determine that the defendant is no longer impaired, unless there is evidence that the defendant is still impaired from a combination of alcohol and drugs.[213]

ix. Release from detention

A magistrate must release a defendant from the impaired driving detention if

　　1. the maximum twenty-four-hour period for the detention has expired;

---

207. G.S. 15A-534.2(c).

208. State v. Labinski, 188 N.C. App. 120, 127 n.4 (2008).

209. G.S. 15A-534.2(b).

210. G.S. 15A-534.2(c).

211. G.S. 15A-534.2(d).

212. *Id.; see generally* Shea Denning, *Magistrate Procedures for Ordering Civil License Revocations and the Seizure and Impoundment of Motor Vehicles*, ADMIN. OF J. BULL. No. 2013/01, Feb. 2013, at 3–4 (discussing the instruments used for chemical analysis), http://sogpubs.unc.edu/electronicversions/pdfs/aojb1301.pdf.

213. G.S. 15A-534.2(d).

2. the defendant's physical and mental faculties are no longer impaired to the extent that the defendant presents a danger of physical injury to the defendant or others or of damage to property; *or*
3. if a sober, responsible adult appears and is willing and able to take custody of the defendant until the defendant's physical and mental faculties are no longer impaired so as to present a danger of physical injury to the defendant or others or of damage to property.[214]

Form AOC-CR-270 should be used to effectuate the release, checking the appropriate box under the section titled "Release from Detention Order." Note that if the release is to a sober, responsible adult, that person's name should be listed on the form, and he or she should sign where indicated. Also note that a release to a sober, responsible adult for this purpose is not the same as a custody release, discussed in section III.C.1.b, above. In a custody release, the custodian agrees to supervise the defendant while on pretrial release; the sober responsible adult merely agrees to take custody of the defendant until he or she is no longer impaired so as to present a danger of injury or damage. Finally, the fact that the impaired driving detention ends does not mean that the defendant can be released on pretrial release; even if one of the events listed above occurs, the defendant still must satisfy any conditions of pretrial release that have been set in the release order before he or she can be released on pretrial release.

c. ICE detainer

As discussed in section II.H, above, the fact that an Immigration and Customs Enforcement (ICE) detainer is in place is not a reason to delay the initial appearance or the setting of conditions of pretrial release. The ICE detainer requests that the jailer hold the named person for up to forty-eight hours after the person would otherwise be released so that ICE can take custody of the person. When such a detainer is in place and the jailer complies with the request, the person will not be immediately released even if he or she satisfies the conditions of release (e.g., a $1,000 secured bond).

G. Modification of Conditions

A magistrate may modify his or her pretrial release order at any time before the first appearance before a district court judge.[215] If a magistrate believes there are compelling reasons to modify another magistrate's pretrial release order, it is best, if possible, to consult with the other magistrate before making the modification. As a general rule, once the first appearance has occurred, the case is within the judge's jurisdiction and only a judge can modify the bond. There are, however, two important exceptions to this general rule. First, if a judge issues an OFA—for example, for failure to appear—the magistrate has jurisdiction to set conditions. The second situation when a magistrate may modify a bond after a defendant has appeared in court is when a defendant has been arrested by an officer for violating a pretrial release order. Officers have authority to arrest in these situations under G.S. 15A-401(b)(2)f, and such an arrest triggers the requirements of an initial appearance.[216]

---

214. G.S. 15A-534.2(c).
215. G.S. 15A-534(e).
216. G.S. 15A-501(2); -511(a)(1).

Figure 9. Surrender by Surety

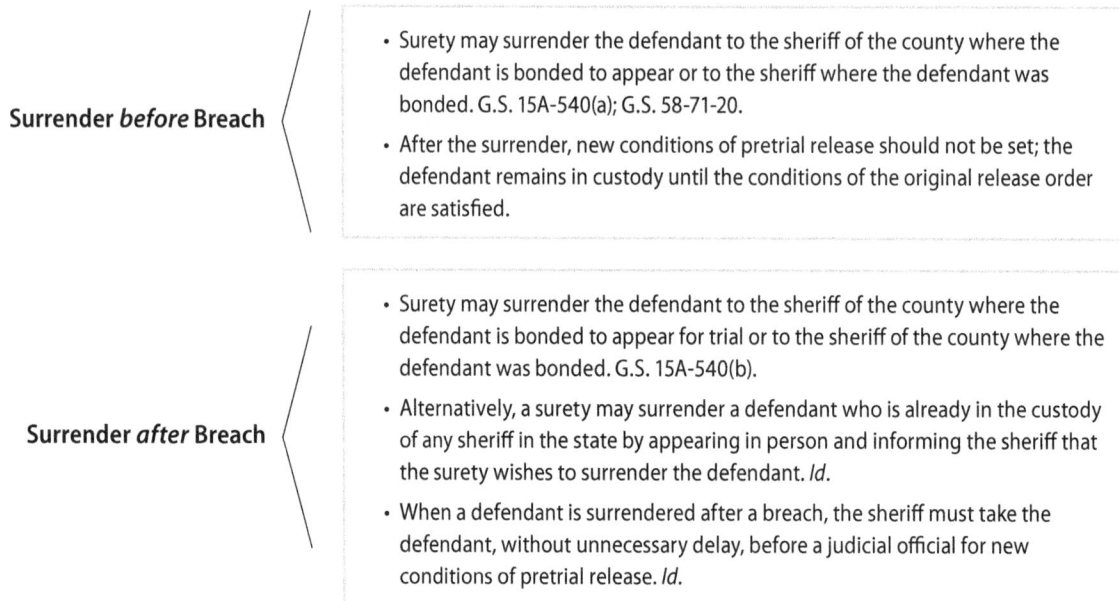

Surrender *before* Breach

- Surety may surrender the defendant to the sheriff of the county where the defendant is bonded to appear or to the sheriff where the defendant was bonded. G.S. 15A-540(a); G.S. 58-71-20.
- After the surrender, new conditions of pretrial release should not be set; the defendant remains in custody until the conditions of the original release order are satisfied.

Surrender *after* Breach

- Surety may surrender the defendant to the sheriff of the county where the defendant is bonded to appear for trial or to the sheriff of the county where the defendant was bonded. G.S. 15A-540(b).
- Alternatively, a surety may surrender a defendant who is already in the custody of any sheriff in the state by appearing in person and informing the sheriff that the surety wishes to surrender the defendant. *Id.*
- When a defendant is surrendered after a breach, the sheriff must take the defendant, without unnecessary delay, before a judicial official for new conditions of pretrial release. *Id.*

H. Term of the Bond

A defendant is covered by a bond until judgment is entered in district court from which no appeal is taken, or until judgment is entered in superior court.[217] However, the bond ends earlier if

1. a judge releases the obligor from the bond,
2. the defendant is properly surrendered by a surety,
3. the proceeding is terminated by voluntary dismissal by the state before forfeiture is ordered, or
4. an indefinite prayer for judgment continued has been entered in district court.[218]

I. Surrender of Defendant by Surety

A surety may arrest a defendant for the purpose of surrender.[219] Although G.S. 58-71-30 permits a magistrate to issue an OFA for a defendant when a surety makes a written request on a certified copy of the bond, a magistrate should not do so without consulting with his or her chief district court judge or senior resident superior court judge. It ordinarily would not be a good practice to issue an OFA under such circumstances; this is additionally true as G.S. 58-71-30 may conflict with G.S. 15A-305, which only authorizes the issuance of an OFA on certain grounds. Note that G.S. 58-71-195 provides that if there is a conflict between the provisions of G.S. Chapter 58 and G.S. Chapter 15A, the provisions of G.S. Chapter 15A govern. The procedures for surrendering a defendant vary depending on whether the surrender is done before or after a breach of conditions of a bail bond. Figure 9 presents the relevant rules.

---

217. G.S. 15A-534(h).
218. *Id.*
219. G.S. 15A-540; G.S. 58-71-30.

IV. Fugitives

A. Generally

Extradition is the procedure by which a person who has committed a crime in one state, escaped from prison in one state, or violated probation or parole imposed by one state and has fled to another state is returned to the first state. For more information about extradition, see ROBERT L. FARB, STATE OF NORTH CAROLINA EXTRADITION MANUAL (UNC SCHOOL OF GOVERNMENT, 3d ed. 2013) (hereinafter EXTRADITION MANUAL), from which most of the text in this section is drawn directly. Note that separate procedures apply to defendants who violate probation imposed by another state and are in North Carolina pursuant to a supervision agreement under the Interstate Compact for Adult Offender Supervision (Interstate Compact). In those cases, the Interstate Compact rules, discussed in section III.A.2.l, above, apply. When a defendant has violated probation imposed by another state and is found in North Carolina with no Interstate Compact supervision agreement in place, extradition rules govern the process for returning the defendant to the other state.

Most commonly, magistrates will deal with fugitives from other states who are found in North Carolina. Consider the case of a person who committed a crime—say, armed robbery—in Ohio and fled to North Carolina. Probably the person already has been charged formally in Ohio, either by indictment or by an arrest warrant. When he or she is discovered in North Carolina, the person may be arrested by a North Carolina officer, either with or without an arrest warrant from a North Carolina magistrate. The sections below discuss the procedures that apply in these circumstances. See section IV.C, below, for a discussion of the magistrate's involvement when a fugitive from North Carolina is found in another state.

B. Fugitive from Another State Found in North Carolina

1. Warrantless Arrest by Officer

When a fugitive from another state is found in North Carolina, an officer may arrest the fugitive without a warrant *only if*

1. the person has been charged with a crime in the other state *and*
2. the charged crime is punishable there by death or more than one year's imprisonment.

After arresting without a warrant, the officer must take the fugitive before a North Carolina magistrate as soon as possible. The magistrate must then determine whether the officer had authority to make the warrantless arrest. The question for the magistrate is whether the person has been charged in the other state, not whether there was probable cause to charge. The officer's information must be reliable; it can be a DCI message, or it may be a letter, email, facsimile, or telephone call from an officer in the other state.

When an officer brings a fugitive to a magistrate after making a warrantless arrest, the magistrate should follow the procedures illustrated in Figure 10.

Figure 10.   Magistrate Procedure: Fugitive from Another State Arrested on a Warrantless Arrest

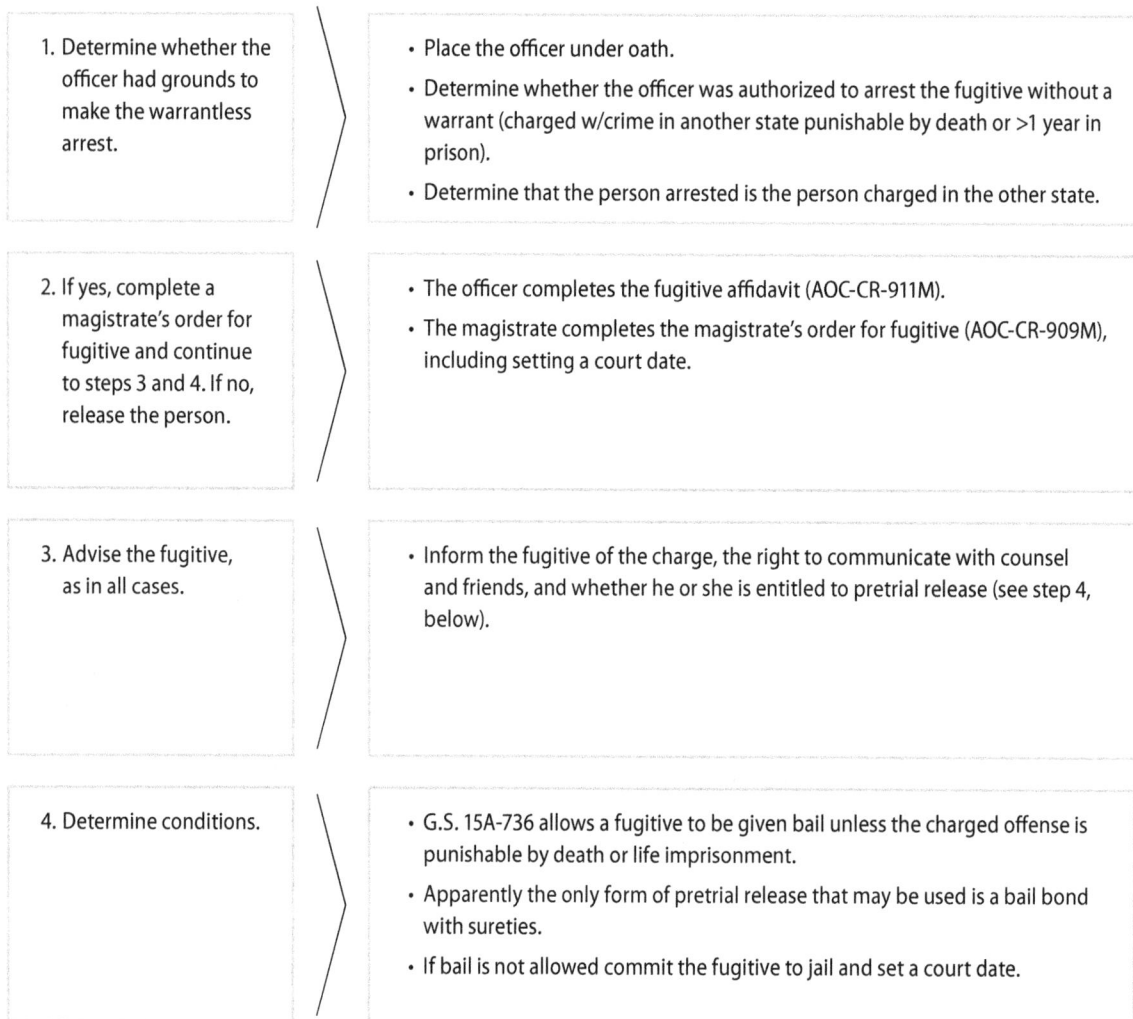

1. Determine whether the officer had grounds to make the warrantless arrest.	• Place the officer under oath. • Determine whether the officer was authorized to arrest the fugitive without a warrant (charged w/crime in another state punishable by death or >1 year in prison). • Determine that the person arrested is the person charged in the other state.
2. If yes, complete a magistrate's order for fugitive and continue to steps 3 and 4. If no, release the person.	• The officer completes the fugitive affidavit (AOC-CR-911M). • The magistrate completes the magistrate's order for fugitive (AOC-CR-909M), including setting a court date.
3. Advise the fugitive, as in all cases.	• Inform the fugitive of the charge, the right to communicate with counsel and friends, and whether he or she is entitled to pretrial release (see step 4, below).
4. Determine conditions.	• G.S. 15A-736 allows a fugitive to be given bail unless the charged offense is punishable by death or life imprisonment. • Apparently the only form of pretrial release that may be used is a bail bond with sureties. • If bail is not allowed commit the fugitive to jail and set a court date.

2. Officer's Request for Fugitive Warrant

Sometimes an officer will come to a magistrate for a North Carolina fugitive arrest warrant, called a Fugitive Warrant, before arresting a fugitive from another state who has been found in North Carolina. The form for a Fugitive Warrant is AOC-CR-910M. A magistrate is authorized to issue such a warrant in only three situations:

1. the person is charged with a crime in another state and has fled,
2. the person was convicted of a crime in another state and has fled to avoid sentencing or has escaped from imprisonment, *or*
3. the person was convicted of a crime in another state and has violated probation, parole, or post-release supervision by fleeing.

The officer's information must be reliable; it may be from a DCI message or a letter, email, facsimile, or telephone call. The magistrate's job is not to determine whether there is probable cause to believe the person committed the crime; the magistrate only determines that one of the three grounds for arrest exist. Figure 11 illustrates the procedure to be followed in these circumstances.

Figure 11.   Magistrate Procedure: Officer's Request for a Fugitive Warrant

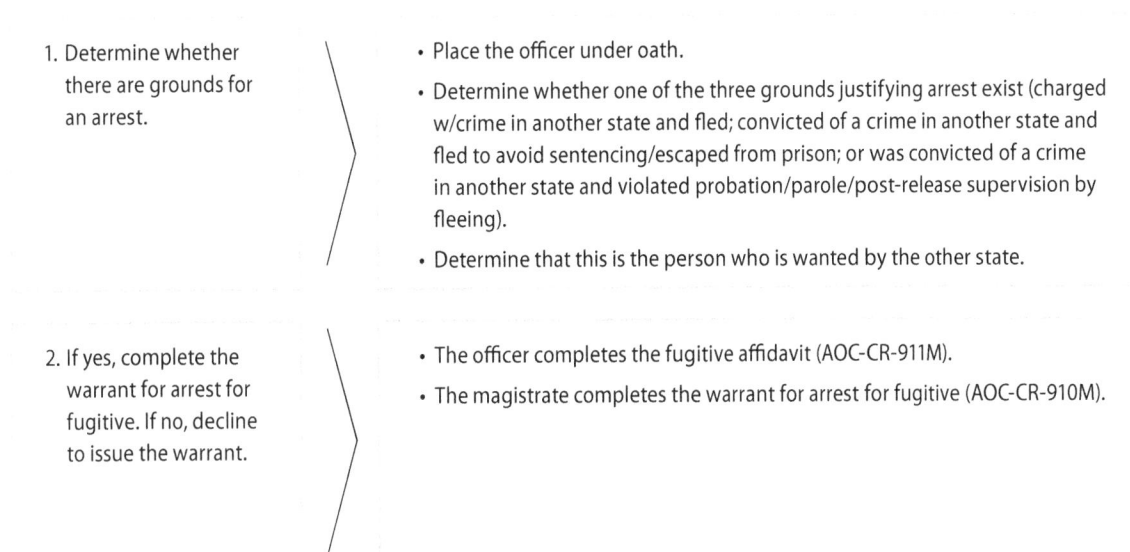

1. Determine whether there are grounds for an arrest.	• Place the officer under oath. • Determine whether one of the three grounds justifying arrest exist (charged w/crime in another state and fled; convicted of a crime in another state and fled to avoid sentencing/escaped from prison; or was convicted of a crime in another state and violated probation/parole/post-release supervision by fleeing). • Determine that this is the person who is wanted by the other state.
2. If yes, complete the warrant for arrest for fugitive. If no, decline to issue the warrant.	• The officer completes the fugitive affidavit (AOC-CR-911M). • The magistrate completes the warrant for arrest for fugitive (AOC-CR-910M).

Once the fugitive warrant is issued, the officer makes the arrest and takes the defendant before a magistrate as soon as possible for the setting of pretrial conditions, just as would be done for a North Carolina crime. When an officer arrests a fugitive on the basis of a warrant and brings the fugitive before a magistrate, the magistrate should inform the fugitive of the charges, determine whether to allow bail, etc., as described in steps 3–4 of Figure 10.

3. Fugitive Who Has Not Been Charged

Another possibility, though unusual, is that the person has not yet been formally charged in the other state. For example, a person may have robbed a convenience store in Virginia late at night and fled to North Carolina, during which time no warrant was issued because no judicial official was on duty in Virginia.

The extradition statutes allow a fugitive to be arrested in North Carolina even though the fugitive has not yet been formally charged in the other state. However, the officer may do so only with an arrest warrant. The procedure for issuing such a warrant is the same as that for charging someone with a North Carolina crime; that is, the officer must be placed under oath and must state facts from which the magistrate can independently determine that there is probable cause to believe that the person committed the crime in another state. A magistrate cannot simply accept the word of the officers from the other state that the person committed the crime; the magistrate must be told the reasons for reaching that conclusion. Note that this is different from other situations involving a fugitive in which the magistrate need only establish that the person has been charged in the other state.

If the magistrate determines that there is probable cause, the magistrate should issue an arrest warrant. The standard arrest warrant form will need to be modified to indicate that the crime is one committed against the law of another state. The magistrate does not need to spell out the elements of the offense but simply can state the name of the other state's crime. The name of the crime given by the officers from that state should be used, even if it is different from the name used in North Carolina (for example, "second degree robbery"). After the warrant is issued, the case proceeds like any other involving a fugitive.

Figure 12.   Magistrate Procedure: Governor's Warrant

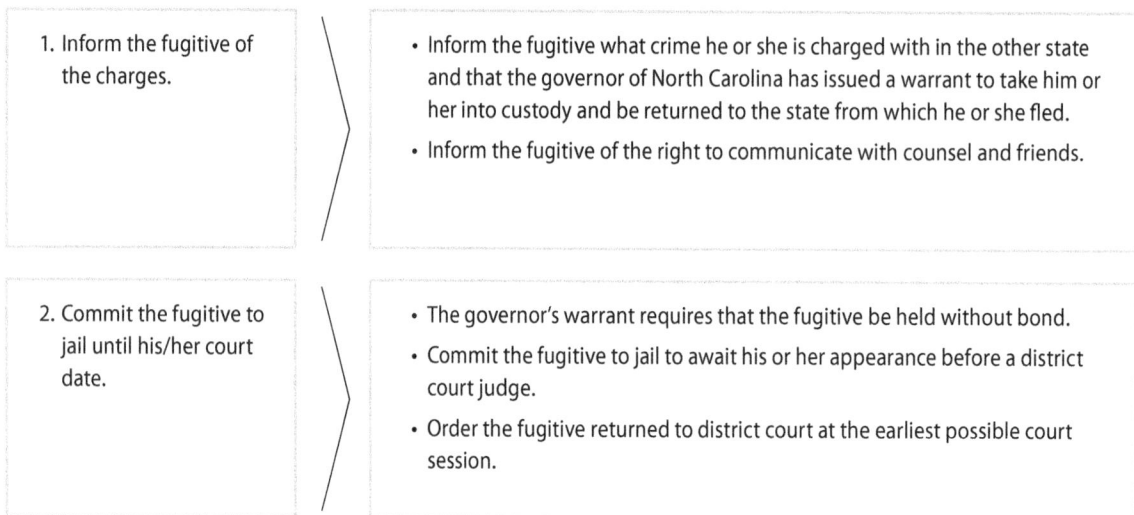

1. Inform the fugitive of the charges.	• Inform the fugitive what crime he or she is charged with in the other state and that the governor of North Carolina has issued a warrant to take him or her into custody and be returned to the state from which he or she fled. • Inform the fugitive of the right to communicate with counsel and friends.
2. Commit the fugitive to jail until his/her court date.	• The governor's warrant requires that the fugitive be held without bond. • Commit the fugitive to jail to await his or her appearance before a district court judge. • Order the fugitive returned to district court at the earliest possible court session.

4. Governor's Warrant

Once arrested, a fugitive is held until formal extradition procedures can take place. If he or she wishes to do so, the fugitive may waive extradition before a clerk of court or a judge and immediately be released to the state from which the fugitive fled. Many fugitives, knowing they will be extradited and not wanting to spend the time required for formal extradition, choose to do this.

If the fugitive does not waive extradition, the state from which the fugitive fled must formally request the governor of North Carolina to extradite. If the governor decides to extradite, a governor's warrant will be issued. A governor's warrant authorizes the taking of the fugitive into custody—in fact, the fugitive already may be in custody if he or she was not allowed bail or could not make bail—to be turned over to an agent of the other state.

When a fugitive is brought before a magistrate on a governor's warrant, the magistrate should follow the procedure outlined in Figure 12.

C. Fugitives from North Carolina Found in Another State

If a person who committed a crime in North Carolina flees to another state and is found there, a similar procedure takes place. Once the fugitive is arrested in the other state, a North Carolina district attorney or assistant district attorney of the county where the fugitive is charged is notified and must put together the documents that the North Carolina governor's office will need in requesting extradition (assuming that the fugitive does not waive extradition).

Magistrates only are involved in extraditing a fugitive from North Carolina who has fled to another state if an arrest warrant is used as the charging document. If so, the warrant must be accompanied by an affidavit (usually by the investigating officer or the victim) stating the grounds for charging the defendant. This affidavit must be sworn to before a magistrate or judge and should have the same date as the warrant (or earlier). Some states will not extradite if the date of the affidavit (for example, January 25, 2014) is later than the date of the arrest warrant (for example, January 20, 2014). Therefore, when a warrant is issued without an accompanying affidavit (oral sworn testimony is sufficient to support an arrest warrant in North Carolina), a new arrest warrant must be issued when the affidavit is prepared so that the dates of the arrest warrant and the affidavit will be the same. In addition, the extradition process for fugitives from North Carolina found in another state may require certification of documents by judicial officials. These requirements are discussed in detail in the EXTRADITION MANUAL.

V. Search Warrants

A. Generally

A search warrant directs a law enforcement officer to search premises, vehicles, persons, or other places and to seize specified items or persons.[220] Any item is subject to seizure under a search warrant if there is probable cause to believe it

- is stolen or embezzled,
- is contraband or otherwise unlawfully possessed,
- has been used or is possessed for the purpose of being used to commit or conceal the commission of a crime, *or*
- is evidence of an offense or the identity of a person participating in an offense.[221]

Typically, officers need a search warrant to seize items. Sometimes, however, they need a search warrant to seize a person—for example, when the officers have a warrant to arrest a person but the person is inside a friend's house and the friend will not allow the officers to enter.

This section focuses on a magistrate's role in issuing search warrants. For an extensive discussion of search warrants, including, among other issues, the advantages of using them and the consequences of unlawful searches, see ARREST, SEARCH, AND INVESTIGATION.[222]

Two basic documents are used for search warrants. First, the application for the warrant; second, the warrant itself. Form AOC-CR-119 contains a generic application (on one side) and a generic warrant (on the other side). A special form, AOC-CR-155, is used for search warrants to seize blood or urine in impaired driving cases.

B. The Officer's Application

1. Generally

An application for a search warrant must be in writing upon oath or affirmation.[223] All applications must contain

1. the name and title of the applicant;
2. a statement that there is probable cause to believe that the items subject to seizure may be found in or upon a designated or described place, vehicle, or person;
3. allegations of fact supporting the statement (the statement must be supported by one or more affidavits setting forth the facts and circumstances establishing probable cause

---

220. G.S. 15A-241.
221. G.S. 15A-242.
222. ROBERT L. FARB, ARREST, SEARCH, AND INVESTIGATION IN NORTH CAROLINA (UNC School of Government, 4th ed. 2011).
223. G.S. 15A-244.

to believe that the items are in the places or in the possession of the individuals to be searched); *and*

4. a request that the court issue a search warrant directing a search for and seizure of the items in question.[224]

The AOC forms noted above have sections for all of these required elements.

2. Name of Applicant

The first item on the application form is the name and address of the person applying for the warrant or, if the person applying for the warrant is an officer, the officer's name, rank, and agency. Although people who are not law enforcement officers legally may apply for a search warrant,[225] most commonly an officer will apply. It is recommended that magistrates get guidance from their chief district court judge or senior resident superior court judge on handling applications for search warrants by private persons.

3. Description of Person or Property to Be Seized

The application form provides space for a listing of the property to be seized or the person to be arrested. The officer who executes a search warrant need not be the officer who applies for the warrant. Therefore, the description of the property to be seized must be sufficiently detailed so that an officer executing the search warrant does not seize the wrong property. The subsections below provide more detail on how the property or person to be seized should be described.

a. Property. The more common the property, the more detailed the description must be to avoid seizure of the wrong thing. Thus, "stolen gun" and "refrigerator" are not sufficient. When dealing with common items, including the serial number, brand, model, and visual description of an item to be seized would be helpful identifying information. A detailed description is less important for obvious contraband, such as a machine gun or non-tax-paid liquor. Moreover, an officer may seize obvious contraband not described in the affidavit, if seen in plain view or seized incident to arrest. Not much detail is needed if the property is drugs, which ordinarily may not be possessed lawfully. Although it is best to state the name of the drug, the generic name is adequate. It is not necessary to state the amount of illegal drugs being sought.

b. Person. As noted above, there are situations when an officer will be required to obtain a search warrant to enter premises to make an arrest with an arrest warrant or an OFA. In such a case, the officer must describe the person to be seized by giving that person's name and description. If the person's name is known, only the name is required; a physical description can be helpful or can be a substitute for the name if the name is unknown (e.g., "white male, 6'5", long blond hair and mustache").

4. Crime Committed

The next item on the application form is the crime at issue. It is useful to give a short phrase describing the crime, such as "possession of marijuana," "armed robbery," or "felonious breaking or entering." It is best to avoid abbreviations such as "A/R" or "FB/E" because they cause confusion.

The description of the crime need not be as detailed as in criminal process, because a person is not being charged with a crime by this document. In fact, it is possible that a person whose property is being searched may have nothing to do with the crime under investigation.

---

224. *Id.*

225. *In re* 1990 Red Cherokee Jeep, VIN 1J4FJ38L4LL146261, 131 N.C. App. 108, 112–13 (1998).

5. What Is to Be Searched

The application form requires that the applicant specify and describe where the person or item sought is located. The options on the form include "premises," "person(s)," "vehicle(s)," and "other places or items." The application may specify any combination of these locations, if justified by the facts. As noted above, the officer who executes a search warrant need not be the officer who applies for the warrant. Therefore, the descriptions of the premises, persons, vehicles, or other places or items to be searched must be sufficiently detailed so that an officer executing the search warrant does not search the wrong person or property.

a. Premises. If the premises are a house, the street number is sufficient. However, it is best to include a physical description in case the street number is wrong. If the street number is wrong but the officer searches the correct house based on the physical description, the search warrant still would be valid. If the house and street numbers are incorrect and the application contains no description, the warrant will be invalid. If the premises are an apartment, the form should give the apartment number or a description of its location within the apartment complex. Magistrates should remember that an officer unfamiliar with the investigation must be able to find the premises based on the description in the application.

A search warrant to search premises does not give authority to search persons on the premises at the time of the search, except as provided in G.S. 15A-256. Thus, if particular suspects are involved and evidence may be hidden on them, the search warrant should authorize a search of them under the "person(s)" block. If a search of such persons is not authorized, officers can detain them (and frisk them for weapons, if appropriate) only while searching the premises. If the search of the premises fails to uncover items being searched for, the officers can then conduct a full search of such persons. Because no North Carolina appellate case has considered the practice, magistrates should be cautious about authorizing a search of "all persons on the premises."[226]

If a search warrant authorizes only a search of the premises, courts have ruled in certain circumstances that officers may search a vehicle on the premises (if the vehicle might contain evidence described in the application) when the officer knows the vehicle belongs to the suspect whose premises are being searched. However, to avoid any question of lawfulness, and also to authorize search of the vehicle if it is found away from the premises, a search warrant should authorize search of vehicles under the "vehicle(s)" block, if there is probable cause that the items sought might be in the vehicle.

Although usually not legally required, a description of the outbuildings on the premises that the officer wants to search is useful, or the application might simply state "outbuildings on the premises."

b. Persons. When listing persons, the application should include the person's name, age, height, weight, race, distinguishing marks, and so forth.

c. Vehicles. When listing vehicles, the application should include model, make, year, color, license tag, and anything else that distinguishes it from other similar vehicles, such as its vehicle identification number (VIN), if known.

d. Other places or items to be searched. This category may be used when the place or item to be searched is not in the premises or vehicles or on a person. For example, an officer may need a search warrant to search luggage that the officer has seized in a situation when a warrantless search cannot be made.

---

226. Jeff Welty, *Search Warrants for "All Persons on the Premises,"* North Carolina Criminal Law blog (Nov. 25, 2009), http://nccriminallaw.sog.unc.edu/?p=889.

Figure 13. Application for Search Warrant (AOC-CR-119) (Rev. 6/12)

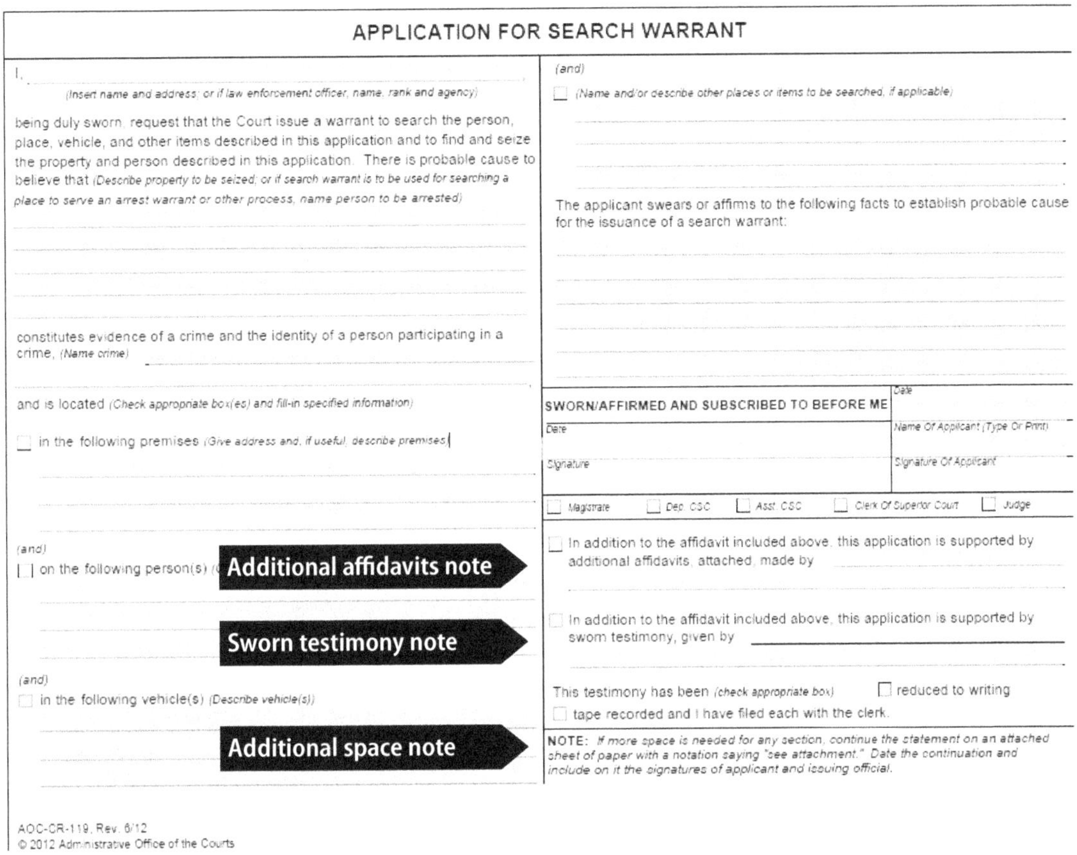
APPLICATION FOR SEARCH WARRANT

I, (Insert name and address; or if law enforcement officer, name, rank and agency)

being duly sworn, request that the Court issue a warrant to search the person, place, vehicle, and other items described in this application and to find and seize the property and person described in this application. There is probable cause to believe that (Describe property to be seized; or if search warrant is to be used for searching a place to serve an arrest warrant or other process, name person to be arrested)

constitutes evidence of a crime and the identity of a person participating in a crime, (Name crime)

and is located (Check appropriate box(es) and fill-in specified information)

☐ in the following premises (Give address and, if useful, describe premises)

(and)

☐ on the following person(s)

(and)

☐ in the following vehicle(s) (Describe vehicle(s))

(and)

☐ (Name and/or describe other places or items to be searched, if applicable)

The applicant swears or affirms to the following facts to establish probable cause for the issuance of a search warrant:

SWORN/AFFIRMED AND SUBSCRIBED TO BEFORE ME

Date | Signature | Date | Name Of Applicant (Type Or Print) | Signature Of Applicant

☐ Magistrate ☐ Dep. CSC ☐ Asst. CSC ☐ Clerk Of Superior Court ☐ Judge

☐ In addition to the affidavit included above, this application is supported by additional affidavits, attached, made by

☐ In addition to the affidavit included above, this application is supported by sworn testimony, given by

This testimony has been (check appropriate box) ☐ reduced to writing ☐ tape recorded and I have filed each with the clerk.

NOTE: If more space is needed for any section, continue the statement on an attached sheet of paper with a notation saying "see attachment." Date the continuation and include on it the signatures of applicant and issuing official.

AOC-CR-119, Rev. 6/12
© 2012 Administrative Office of the Courts

6. Statement of Facts Establishing Probable Cause

The application provides space to list the facts that establish probable cause for the issuance of the search warrant. This portion of the form is where the applicant provides the required supporting affidavit.

a. When additional space is needed. If all of the facts establishing probable cause do not fit on the form, additional sheets may be attached. At the very bottom of the application form, a note says: "If more space is needed for any section, continue the statement on an attached sheet of paper with a notation saying 'see attachment.' Date the continuation and include on it the signatures of applicant and issuing official."[227] It is important to follow this procedure so that later there is no question as to whether the attachments were part of the original application. It is also a good idea to include a title on the attachment, such as "In the Matter of Murder of Steve Jones," and to staple the additional sheets to the form.

b. Additional affidavits. In some cases, affidavits by people other than the officer applying for the warrant may be submitted to support the warrant. For example, the officer may provide affidavits by other officers or by an informant. When this happens, the magistrate should check the box on the form that says "In addition to the affidavit included above, this application is supported by

227. See Figure 13.

additional affidavits, attached, made by _____,"[228] and fill in the person's name and address or, if the person is a law enforcement officer, name, rank, and agency. The additional affidavits should be dated and clearly marked as attachments to the application.

c. Additional testimony establishing probable cause. In some cases, in addition to the affidavit, a person will provide sworn testimony setting out the facts establishing probable cause. When this happens, the magistrate should check the box on the form that says "In addition to the affidavit included above, this application is supported by sworn testimony, given by _____,"[229] and fill in the person's name and address. Testimony given in this way should be reduced to writing or tape-recorded and filed with the clerk.[230] The magistrate should check the appropriate box on the form to indicate whether the testimony has been reduced to writing or tape-recorded.

If the officer believes it is important to exclude some supporting information from the suspect's copy of the application (e.g., to keep information from a suspect that might reveal an informant's identity), the officer may wish to have the informant's testimony tape-recorded and filed with the clerk.

d. General rules for the affidavit. The most common problem with search warrants is that the application fails to contain enough of the information known by the officer. When preparing the statement of facts establishing probable cause[231] it usually is best for the officer to write a statement clearly outlining the succession of events in chronological order. The statement should include an explanation of what led the officer to conclude that the evidence sought is related to a crime and why the officer believes the evidence can be found where he or she wants to search.

There are no set rules about what needs to be in the statement. A good statement need not have an informant's report. On the other hand, a good statement could consist solely of an informant's report, though it is better if the officer corroborates some of the informant's information. What is important is whether all the facts stated together establish a fair probability that the evidence is where the officer wants to search. Reliable hearsay, such as information obtained from another officer or a reliable informant, is permitted.

If information from a confidential informant is used, it is helpful if the confidential informant's report shows how the informant got the information (e.g., the informant was at the scene or someone told the informant) and why the informant should be believed (has given good information before, for example; the report should provide details regarding the information previously provided such as when the information was provided, how often, and whether it resulted in arrests or convictions). An officer's corroboration (through personal knowledge or reliable hearsay) of a confidential informant's report adds weight to the report. It is not necessary to establish that an identified, reliable citizen informant has previously given good information to the police.

Personal observations should be stated in such a way that it is clear that the officer is the person making the observation. Including truthful phrases like "I saw . . . " or "Affiant saw . . . " is a helpful way of doing this.

---

228. See Figure 13.

229. See Figure 13.

230. *But see* State v. Hicks, 60 N.C. App. 116, 121 (1982) (warrant not fatal where magistrate did not check the box on the form and placed relied upon notes in the magistrate's desk drawer; notes were never filed with the clerk).

231. See section I.B.3.b (discussing the meaning of probable cause).

7. Signatures

The officer applying for a search warrant must sign the application under oath or affirmation.[232] There is a place on the application form for the officer's signature and for the magistrate to sign and date the form to indicate that the officer's statement was sworn.

C. Issuance of a Search Warrant

1. Authority to Issue

Only judicial officials may issue search warrants.[233] Appellate justices and judges and superior court judges may issue search warrants to search throughout North Carolina.[234] District court judges are limited to searches within their respective judicial districts.[235] Clerks and magistrates are limited to searches within their counties.[236] One magistrate can issue a search warrant even if another magistrate has refused to do so under the same factual circumstances. However, the second magistrate should view the first magistrate's refusal as a cautionary signal.

2. Examination of the Applicant

When an officer applies for a search warrant the magistrate may examine the officer and/or other witnesses under oath or affirmation to determine that probable cause exists to issue the warrant.[237] Information supporting the issuance of a search warrant may be offered by oral testimony under oath or affirmation presented to the issuing judicial official by a sworn law enforcement officer by means of an audio and video transmission in which both parties can see and hear each other. Before this method can be used, the procedures and type of equipment to be used for audio and video transmission must be submitted to the AOC by the senior resident superior court judge and the chief district court judge for a judicial district and approved by the AOC.[238]

3. Probable Cause Determination

The magistrate must make an independent judgment as to the existence of probable cause.[239] The magistrate must be told the facts that support the officer's conclusion that probable cause exists; for example, simply stating the officer's or informant's conclusion that drugs are in a particular apartment is not sufficient. The magistrate must determine that there is probable cause—a fair probability—that the items or persons sought are in the places to be searched.

As described above, sometimes the applicant will offer additional affidavits or additional sworn testimony. These additional materials may be considered if they have been properly attached to the affidavit, reduced to writing, or tape-recorded. At a hearing to suppress evidence seized pursuant

---

232. G.S. 15A-245(a).

233. G.S. 15A-243.

234. G.S. 15A-243(a).

235. G.S. 15A-243(b)(1).

236. G.S. 15A-243(b)(2)–(3) (incorporating by reference provisions of G.S. Chapter 7A limiting search warrant authority to searches within the official's county).

237. G.S. 15A-245.

238. G.S. 15A- 245(a)(3).

239. See section I.B.3.b (discussing the meaning of probable cause).

to a search warrant, only affidavits attached to the application or sworn testimony reduced to writing or tape-recorded and filed with the clerk may be considered. Other information told or given to the magistrate is inadmissible at the hearing.

4. Modification

Once a search warrant has been issued and changes need to be made to it, it is better to issue a new warrant and have the first warrant returned unexecuted.

Appendix: Outline of Procedures for Taking Bail Bonds

MEMORANDUM

DATE: May 2013

FROM: Troy D. Page, Assistant Legal Counsel, North Carolina Administrative Office of the Courts

Note: For additional guidance on taking secured bonds see JOAN G. BRANNON & ANN M. ANDERSON, NORTH CAROLINA CLERK OF SUPERIOR COURT PROCEDURES MANUAL, Chapter 22 (UNC School of Government, 2012).

I. Generally

A. After defendant's conditions of release have been established, a judicial official "must effect the release of that person upon satisfying himself that the conditions of release have been met." G.S. 15A-537(a). This includes meeting any monetary condition of release by the posting of an appearance bond.

B. Non-monetary Conditions of Release Do Not Require an Appearance Bond.
   1. Written promises to appear and custody releases are "satisfied" by the signature(s) of the defendant and the custodian agreeing to supervise the defendant on the Conditions of Release and Release Order (AOC-CR-200).
   2. Post-release conditions on the defendant's conduct (*e.g.*, "stay away from the victim") are not part of the bail bond posted for the defendant's release and therefore are not included on the Appearance Bond for Pretrial Release (AOC-CR-201, hereafter Appearance Bond).
   3. Although house arrest with electronic monitoring (FHA), G.S. 15A-534(a)(5), is a non-monetary condition of release, the imposition of EHA as a condition of release also requires imposition of a secured bond. Therefore, a defendant whose conditions of release include EHA also must execute an Appearance Bond to satisfy the secured bond before being released.

C. Monetary Conditions of Release <u>Always</u> Require an Appearance Bond.
   1. "An appearance bond is a contract of the defendant and the surety with the State." *State v. Corl*, 58 N.C. App. 107, 111 (1982).
   2. Whether secured or unsecured, a bond promising forfeiture of money to the State upon defendant's failure to appear must be executed on an Appearance Bond specifying the terms of forfeiture.
   3. The Release Order does not specify the terms of forfeiture, so a Release Order by itself is insufficient to obligate the defendant or a surety on a monetary bond. Without an Appearance Bond there is no contract from which to enforce the obligation to appear through forfeiture.
   4. Because the defendant, as principal, always is liable for forfeiture of a monetary bond, the defendant <u>always</u> must sign the Appearance Bond, even if the bond is secured by a surety's promise or property.

II. Unsecured Bonds

A. An unsecured bond is merely a promise of forfeiture of the defendant's money to the State if the defendant fails to appear as required.

B. There is no requirement that the defendant demonstrate solvency sufficient to satisfy the bond amount; the bond is merely a promise to pay, without any demonstration that the defendant will be able to do so in the event of forfeiture.

C. Defendant still must execute an Appearance Bond to make any eventual forfeiture enforceable.

III. Secured Bonds

A. A secured bond may be satisfied in one of three ways: cash, a mortgage posted pursuant to G.S. 58-74-5, or at least one solvent surety. G.S. 15A-534(a)(4).

B. Cash.
   1. Cash Must Be in the "Full Amount of the Bond." *Id.*
      a. The validity of "splitting" a bond when a portion is fulfilled by cash is unclear, but local practice generally allows it if the local bond policy allows splitting at all.
      b. See section IV for more detail on split bonds.
   2. When "Cash Means Cash."
      a. There is no clear guidance in the statute or appellate case law concerning whether or not a judicial official may specify the type of security that will satisfy a monetary condition of release (*e.g.,* "cash only").
      b. Insurance Companies and Professional Bondsmen May Post Cash Bonds.
         i. If a release order specifies a cash bond, an insurance company bond posted by a bail agent or a bail bond posted by a professional bondsman (personally or through his or her runner) "is considered the same as a cash deposit." G.S. 15A-531(4).
         ii. This rule does not apply to cash bonds in child support contempt cases, for which only actual currency will suffice. *Id.*
   3. Ownership of the Cash (at conclusion of the case).
      a. Cash Deposited by Defendant.
         i. When defendant provides his or her own cash to secure release, the cash remains the defendant's property (unless forfeited). *White v. Ordille*, 229 N.C. 490, 495 (1948).
         ii. The Appearance Bond should be executed in the defendant's name, only.
         iii. **Completing the AOC-CR-201: Cash Bond by Defendant**
            (1) Complete all fields in the form's header.
            (2) Be sure to include <u>all</u> offenses and file numbers for which the bond will secure the defendant's appearance, *i.e.,* the same cases listed on the Release Order.
            (3) Check the box for "☐ **Cash Appearance Bond.**"
            (4) Have the defendant swear or affirm to the bond and sign the bond in the signature field and then complete the section titled "**SWORN AND SUBSCRIBED TO BEFORE ME.**"
            (5) Complete the section titled "**COMPLETE IF CASH DEPOSITED.**"
            (6) Issue the receipt for the cash deposit to the defendant in the defendant's name.

    b.   Cash Deposited by a Third Party.

        i.   The judicial official accepting the bond <u>must</u> determine the third party's intent for disposition of the money.

            (1)   *See* Appearance Bond for Pretrial Release, AOC-CR-201, side two, "**NOTES ON CASH BONDS**," for guidance when determining a third party's intent for the final disposition of the cash.

            (2)   If the third party expects to receive a refund of the money upon conclusion of the defendant's case (assuming there is no forfeiture), the third party <u>must</u> sign the bond as a surety.

- The surety must sign the Appearance Bond as an "Accommodation Bondsman" in order to preserve an ownership interest in the money.
- Cash deposited in this manner will <u>not</u> be available to satisfy any other obligations the defendant may have at the conclusion of the case (*e.g.*, fines and costs).
- **Completing the AOC-CR-201: Cash Bond by Surety**
    - Complete all fields in the form's header.
    - Be sure to include <u>all</u> offenses and file numbers for which the bond will secure the defendant's appearance, *i.e.*, the same cases listed on the Release Order.
    - Check the boxes for "**Surety Appearance Bond**" and "☐ **Cash Deposited By Surety**."
    - Complete all fields under the section titled "**ACCOMMODATION BONDSMAN**" with the surety's information.
    - Have both the defendant and the surety sworn or affirmed to the bond, have both sign the bond in the fields for their signatures, and complete the section titled "**SWORN AND SUBSCRIBED TO BEFORE ME.**"
    - Complete the section titled "**COMPLETE IF CASH DEPOSITED.**"
    - Issue the receipt for the cash deposit to the surety in the surety's name.

            (3)   If the third party wants the money to be available to satisfy the defendant's other obligations in the event of conviction, the third party must <u>not</u> sign the bond.

- The Appearance Bond should be completed as if the cash were deposited by the defendant, as described above.
- The third party effectively has given or loaned the money to the defendant to post as if it was his or her own. The third party will receive neither notice of any forfeiture nor a refund in the event the case is disposed without forfeiture, and any eventual refund of the money will be paid to the defendant.

    4.   Cash Bonds Greater Than $10,000.

Note: *See also*, N.C. Administrative Office of the Courts, Clerk of Superior Court Financial Policies and Procedures 37.11–37.13 (2002).

    a.   Clerks of federal and state courts must report to the Internal Revenue Service (IRS), the federal Financial Crimes Enforcement Network (FinCEN), and certain U.S.

Attorneys when they receive cash in excess of $10,000 as bail for a single defendant. 26 U.S.C. § 6050I(g), 26 C.F.R. § 1.6050I-2, 31 U.S.C. § 5331, and 31 C.F.R. § 1010.331.

 i. Clerks have been required to report cash bail transactions over $10,000 to the IRS for many years.

 ii. The additional requirement to report to the FinCEN was added in 2011 by Pub. L. No. 112-74, § 120, amending 31 U.S.C. § 5331 to require reporting by anyone who "is required to file a report under section 6050I(g) of the Internal Revenue Code," which means the clerks (the only entity covered by subsection (g)).

 iii. The federal regulation adopted in July 2012 to implement the requirement to report to FinCEN, 31 C.F.R. § 1010.331, requires that the clerks report large cash bail transactions in the same form, time, and manner as the IRS report. Therefore, a single IRS Form 8300 (described below) sent to a single IRS address will satisfy both the IRS and the FinCEN reporting requirements.

 iv. In addition to IRS and FinCEN requirements, the clerk is required to report cash bail transactions over $10,000 to the offices of one or more U.S. Attorneys. The clerk must report such transactions to the U.S. Attorney(s) for the jurisdiction(s) where

  (1) the defendant resides and

  (2) where the crime occurred (if different).

 v. The IRS, FinCEN, and U.S. Attorney reports all must be filed by the 15th day after the date the cash bail is received.

b. The reporting requirement applies to magistrates and any other officials who take bonds because they receive cash "on behalf of a clerk," as provided in the federal regulations cited above.

c. Reporting Is Required Only for Certain Specified Criminal Offenses:

- any federal offense involving a controlled substance,
- racketeering,
- money laundering, and
- any substantially similar state offense to those listed above.

d. When to Report a Cash Bond over $10,000.

 i. For the purpose of reporting the cash bond, "cash" means

  (1) actual currency or

  (2) negotiable instruments (*e.g.*, cashier's checks) for $10,000 or <u>less</u>. A negotiable instrument like a cashier's check issued for more than $10,000 is reported independently by the issuing institution, so the IRS and FinCEN do not require duplicate reporting from the clerks.

   Example: Bond is posted with $2,000 in actual currency and a cashier's check for $9,000. This must be reported because the check for less than $10,000 must be counted as cash, thereby making the total exceed $10,000.

   Example: Bond is posted with a single cashier's check for $200,000. This does <u>not</u> need to be reported because a check in that amount is not "cash" for the clerk's reporting purposes.

   Example: Bond is $10,000. Defendant's mother posts $10,000 in actual currency. This does not have to be reported because reporting is required only if the amount posted <u>exceeds</u> $10,000. (But see subsection iii, "Suspicious Transactions," below.)

ii. Aggregating Multiple Payments.

(1) When multiple payments for the defendant's bond exceed the $10,000 threshold, reporting is required.

Example: Defendant's bond is $15,000 for PWISD marijuana. His mother posts $7,500 in cash, and his brother posts the other $7,500. The transaction must be reported because the total cash posted for the defendant on a qualifying offense exceeds $10,000.

(2) Aggregation is not required if the payments are for separate bonds for separate offenses.

Example: Defendant's bond is $9,500 for PWISD marijuana. He has a separate charge of forgery and uttering, with a bond of $5,000. If his mother posts $9,500 in cash for the drug charge and $5,000 in cash for the forgery charge, reporting is not required. However, the magistrate may nonetheless decide to report this bond as a "suspicious transaction"; see subsection iii, below).

(3) The aggregation rule is unclear about related offenses arising from the same event, but the safer course may be to treat multiple charges from the same event as a single offense for reporting purposes.

Example: As the result of a single drug bust, defendant is charged with PWISD marijuana (secured bond of $7,500) and feloniously maintaining a dwelling for the use of controlled substances (secured bond of $5,000). If cash is posted for both bonds, the payment probably should be reported.

iii. Suspicious Transactions. A transaction may be reported if it is suspicious, which the IRS describes as a transaction in which "it appears that a person is trying to cause you not to file Form 8300 or is trying to cause you to file a false or incomplete Form 8300, or if there is a sign of possible illegal activity." I.R.S Publication 1544 (Sept. 2012).

Example: A prospective surety wants to post $25,000 in cash for a defendant's bond. Upon being told that the magistrate must report the transaction, the surety decides to come back later. When he returns, he has a cashier's check for $15,000 and currency of exactly $10,000. This transaction normally would not be reported because the check is not for <u>less</u> than $10,000 and the currency is not <u>more</u> than $10,000. However, because the transaction appears to have been structured for the sole purpose of preventing you from reporting it to the IRS, it should be reported as suspicious.

e. IRS Form 8300.

i. Form 8300 is used to report all qualifying transactions under 26 U.S.C. § 6050I and 31 U.S.C. § 5331.

       (1)   A fillable electronic version of the form and its instructions can be found at www.irs.gov by searching for "Form 8300" in the search field.

       (2)   Additional guidance is found in I.R.S Publication 1544 (Sept. 2012) on the same website (search for "Publication 1544").

ii.   **<u>Willful failure to file Form 8300 for a qualifying transaction is a felony</u>**, 26 U.S.C. § 7203 and 31 U.S.C. § 5322, in addition to civil penalties that may apply.

iii.   Information Required.

       (1)   Complete information is required for both the defendant for whom the bond is posted <u>and</u> any third-party payor.

- Information <u>must</u> be collected from a third party providing the cash, even if that person does not want to sign the Appearance Bond as surety to protect his or her interest in the cash.
- The judicial official accepting the cash <u>must</u> verify the identity of the payor from official documentation. 26 C.F.R. § 1.6050I-2(c)(3)(ii).

       (2)   The Taxpayer Identification Number (TIN) must be collected for both the defendant and any third-party payor.

- If a third party provides the cash, the official taking the bond <u>must</u> collect the third party's TIN, even if that person will not be signing the Appearance Bond as a surety.
- The TIN is one's Social Security Number, if a person has one, and the Individual Taxpayer Identification Number (ITIN) if not.
- The TIN is not required of certain non-resident aliens with limited connections to the United States. The complete list of exceptions is provided in I.R.S. Publication 1544 (Sept. 2012) under the heading "Taxpayer Identification Number (TIN)."

       (3)   Failure to collect complete defendant or payor information will cause the IRS to return Form 8300 to the clerk as deficient, and it can result in monetary penalties for the clerk's office.

iv.   Upon completion, Form 8300 should be filed with the clerk's office along with the magistrate's Off-Site Daily Cash Report.

C. Mortgage.

    1.   A defendant may provide a mortgage to his own real or personal property as security for his bond. G.S. 15A-534(a)(4); G.S. 58-74-5.

       a.   Forfeiture of the bond will be enforceable through sale of the property named in the mortgage, if judgment on the forfeiture remains unsatisfied after execution.

       b.   The defendant still must execute the Appearance Bond for the obligation to be enforceable. The mortgage must be conditioned upon compliance with the bond.

    2.   Although the statute specifies a "mortgage," the standard practice in most counties is to require a deed of trust instead.

       a.   A mortgage is a two-party document, executed by the defendant and payable to the State. Forfeiture of the bond on which the mortgage is conditioned permits the clerk to exercise the power of sale to satisfy any final judgment of forfeiture.

       b.   A deed of trust is a three-party document between the grantor (defendant, in this scenario) and a beneficiary (the State), with power of sale vested in a trustee (the clerk). As with a mortgage, the trustee's power of sale is conditioned upon compliance with the Appearance Bond. If forfeiture occurs and the power of sale must be exercised, the clerk will substitute another party (generally the attorney for the local schools) as trustee to conduct the sale.

3. Affidavit required for mortgage bond.
   a. Unlike a deed of trust, posting an actual mortgage as security for an appearance bond requires that the defendant provide the clerk with "an affidavit of the value of the property mortgaged to be made by at least one witness not interested in the matter, action or proceeding in which the mortgage is given." G.S. 58-74-30.
   b. The statute does not identify any specific person who must execute the affidavit or the basis for the value assessment that must be provided therein, so a magistrate should consult the clerk's office about the requirements for such affidavits, if the charging county's local bond policy allows defendants to post bond by a mortgage (as opposed to a deed of trust).
4. Because G.S. 58-74-5 allows the defendant to post a mortgage for his or her appearance but makes no reference to a surety, a bond posted by an actual mortgage should be to property owned solely by the defendant. (For a deed of trust to property jointly owned by the defendant and another, *e.g.*, a spouse, see "Property owned by defendant and spouse," in section III.D.4.f, below.)
5. **Completing the AOC-CR-201: Bond Secured by Defendant's Mortgage**
   a. Complete all fields in the form's header.
   b. Be sure to include <u>all</u> offenses and file numbers for which the bond will secure the defendant's appearance, *i.e.*, the same cases listed on the Release Order.
   c. Check the box for "☐ **Defendant's Property Appearance Bond**."
   d. Have the defendant swear or affirm to the bond and sign the bond in the signature field and then complete the section titled "**SWORN AND SUBSCRIBED TO BEFORE ME**."
   e. Attach the court's copy of the mortgage document and any supporting documentation (*e.g.*, the affidavit of value) to the court's copy of the Appearance Bond for delivery to the clerk.
D. Surety Bonds.
   1. The Role of the Surety.
      a. A surety is someone who, "with the principal [defendant], is liable for the amount of the bail bond upon forfeiture of bail." G.S. 58-71-1(10).
      b. The surety's obligation is the same as the defendant's: ensuring the defendant's appearance in court. The defendant's failure to appear results in entry of forfeiture against both the defendant and the surety. G.S. 15A-544.3.
   2. Joint and Several Liability with the Defendant.
      a. The surety and defendant are jointly and severally liable for the amount specified in the Appearance Bond. G.S. 15A-544.3(a); G.S. 15A-544.7(a).
         i. <u>All</u> parties who sign the same Appearance Bond are jointly and severally liable for the full amount specified on that bond.
         ii. If local practice permits "splitting" a monetary condition of release among multiple sureties, each surety must sign a <u>separate</u> Appearance Bond for his or her specific portion of the total in order to avoid liability for the entire total.
         iii. The defendant must sign <u>all</u> Appearance Bonds associated with his or her release, regardless of how many are created to satisfy a specific Release Order.
   3. Determining a Surety's Solvency.
      a. When a judicial official takes a surety's bond, "satisfying [himself] whether conditions of release are met includes determining if sureties are sufficiently solvent to meet the bond obligation." G.S. 15A-537(a).
      b. If the determination of the surety's solvency is made in good faith, the judicial official taking the bond may not be held civilly liable for accepting it. *Id.*

     c.   Local considerations for determining a surety's solvency (*e.g.*, the threshold bond amount at which a surety must provide a deed of trust to real property as security) typically are addressed in the local bond policy promulgated by the senior resident superior court judge and the chief district court judge, pursuant to G.S. 15A-535.

4.   Types of Sureties.

     a.   Three entities may serve as surety:
- a professional bondsman, acting personally or through a runner,
- an insurance company, acting through a bail agent, or
- an accommodation bondsman.

         G.S. 15A-531(8).

     b.   Motor Clubs. A fourth entity—a motor club—may post bail bonds in certain limited circumstances. *See* subsection e.iv, below.

     c.   Licensed Sureties. General rules for professional bondsmen and insurance companies.

        i.   Professional bondsmen and insurance companies are licensed to do bail bond business by the Department of Insurance (DOI), as are their agents: runners and bail agents.

            (1)   Runners execute bonds on behalf of professional bondsmen. A runner may work for only one professional bondsman at a time. G.S. 58-71-65(1).

            (2)   Bail agents (also "surety bondsmen") execute bonds on behalf of insurance companies. A bail agent may be an agent of multiple insurance companies at the same time.

            (3)   Runners and bail agents are <u>not</u> sureties. Neither is ever liable to the State for the bond or its forfeiture, and neither may execute a bond other than in the name of their employer.

            (4)   One person may be licensed in multiple roles. Many professional bondsmen and runners also are bail agents for insurance companies.

            (5)   A person may execute a bond *only* in the capacity of a license issued to that person.

> *Example:* Joe holds only a runner's license. He works for a professional bondsman who also is a bail agent for an insurance company. Joe can post bonds only in his capacity as a runner, on behalf of the professional bondsman as surety. Joe <u>cannot</u> execute bonds for the insurance company of which his employer is an agent because Joe himself is not licensed as a bail agent.

        ii.   A licensed surety currently registered with DOI whose license is not suspended, canceled, or revoked may execute bonds in any county in the State. G.S. 58-71-140(e). Bondsmen are no longer required to file their licenses with the clerk of superior court in order to execute bonds in the clerk's county. S.L. 2006-188, § 1.

        iii.   A licensed surety and its agents are prohibited from executing bonds in a county in which the surety has an unsatisfied final judgment of forfeiture. G.S. 15A-544.7(d).

        iv.   A surety's current authorization to execute bonds is reported on the *Surety Report* from the NCAOC's Civil Case Processing System (VCAP).

            (1)   The report is distributed in paper format in some counties, but the most current version is available online at all times at www.nccourts.org/Courts/OCO/Magistrates/Bondsman.

    (2)   If a surety appears on the report for a county, that surety currently is permitted to execute bonds for that county's cases.

- Not all counties print daily copies of the *Surety Report*. If the county prints the report weekly (or less frequently), the online report is a more reliable source of a surety's current status because a surety's status may change daily.
- When taking a bond for another county's case, the judicial official should ensure that the surety appears on the *Surety Report* of the <u>charging</u> county before taking the bond.
- An agent who wishes to execute a bond may do so only if the agent is listed on the current report and is affiliated with the surety on whose behalf the agent wishes to execute the bond.
  - Because a runner may work for only one professional bondsman at a time, the runner will be listed with only one professional bondsman affiliation.
  - Because a bail agent may be affiliated with multiple insurance companies, the judicial official taking the bond should be careful to ensure that the company for whom the agent presents a power of attorney (POA) certificate currently is affiliated with that agent.
- Prohibited sureties are omitted from the report.

    (3)   The NCAOC's Automated Warrant Repository (NCAWARE) relies on the electronic surety registry in VCAP when preparing the Appearance Bond form electronically. A licensed surety currently prohibited from signing bonds will not be available for selection as a surety.

  v.   A surety's appearance on the *Surety Report* is not the sole factor in determining whether or not the surety may execute a bond. Professional bondsmen are limited in the dollar amounts of bonds they can post, and insurance companies limit their agents' authority for a single bond to the amount specified in their POA certificate. See both sections d and e, below.

  vi.   Affidavit required for each bond. G.S. 58-71-140(d).

    (1)   Any licensed surety or agent executing a bond must provide an affidavit detailing any premium or collateral that the surety has received or will receive as compensation for posting the defendant's bond.

    (2)   The affidavit is on side two of the Appearance Bond form, and the surety's or the agent's attestation to the affidavit must be indicated by checking the box immediately under "□ **Surety Appearance Bond**" ("The 'Affidavit' on the reverse side of this Bond is complete and true.") on side one.

    (3)   An accommodation bondsman does not have to provide this affidavit; it is required only for licensed sureties.

  vii.   No blank bonds. A professional bondsman or bail agent may not execute bonds "in blank" for use by another person on the bondsman's behalf. G.S. 58-71-110.

  viii.   Violation of any provision governing licensed sureties in Article 71 of Chapter 58 of the General Statutes is a Class 1 misdemeanor. G.S. 58-71-185.

d.   Professional Bondsmen.

  i.   Personally liable for the bond.

    (1)   Like the defendant, the professional bondsman is personally liable for the bond and any forfeiture thereof.

(2) A professional bondsman is not an incorporated business.
- Any bond executed by the bondsman must be executed in the bondsman's personal name.
- A business name that a bondsman is "doing business as" is not a legal entity that can serve as surety, so such names (*e.g.*, "XYZ Bail Bonds") should <u>not</u> be entered on an Appearance Bond.

(3) A runner executing a bond must provide <u>both</u> his professional bondsman's name and license number <u>and</u> the runner's personal name and license number on the bond.

ii. "Solvency" of a professional bondsman.

(1) A professional bondsman's authority to execute bonds is limited by his deposits of cash and securities, held in trust by the Commissioner of Insurance. G.S. 58-71-145.
- A professional bondsman's securities currently on deposit must equal at least one-eighth of the bondman's total outstanding bonds as of the first day of each month. *Id.*
- A professional bondsman may not execute bonds for a single defendant, whether on a single bond or in the aggregate, that exceed one-fourth of the bondman's total securities on deposit. G.S. 58-71-175.

(2) A professional bondsman whose deposits are deficient (*i.e.*, less than one-eighth of his or her outstanding bonds) may not execute additional bonds until the deficiency is cured. G.S. 58-71-160(a).

(3) As a practical matter, this limitation on professional bondsmen is unenforceable at the time of posting bond because real-time information about a bondsman's current deposits and outstanding liabilities is not yet available to judicial and custodial officials.

iii. **Completing the AOC-CR-201: Bond Secured by Professional Bondsman**

(1) Complete all fields in the form's header.

(2) Be sure to include all offenses and file numbers for which the bond will secure the defendant's appearance, *i.e.*, the same cases listed on the Release Order.

(3) Check the box for "☐ **Surety Appearance Bond**" and the box immediately below it concerning the "Affidavit" on the reverse side of the form.

(4) Complete the fields under **PROFESSIONAL BONDSMAN** with the professional bondsman's name and license number.
- If a runner is executing the bond on behalf of a professional bondsman, <u>both</u> the professional's and the runner's names and license numbers must be entered on the bond.
- For the professional bondsman and any runner executing the bond, enter only their <u>personal</u> names on the bond, not the name of any company under which they conduct business (*e.g.*, "XYZ Bail Bonding"). Professional bondsmen and runners are licensed in their <u>personal</u> capacities, not under a business name.

(5) Attach the bondsman's seal (sticker) to the bond in the space indicated on side two.

(6) Have the professional bondsman or runner complete the **AFFIDAVIT** section on side two.

(7)   Have both the defendant and surety sworn or affirmed to the bond, have both sign the bond in the fields for their signatures, and then complete the section titled "**SWORN AND SUBSCRIBED TO BEFORE ME.**"

e.   Insurance Companies.

    i.   An insurance company executes bonds only through its bail agents ("surety bondsmen"). Only a person currently licensed as a bail agent and registered as an agent of an insurance company may execute bonds on that company's behalf.

    ii.   "Solvency" of an insurance company.

        (1)   Like a professional bondsman, an insurance company doing bail bond business in the State must maintain deposits held in trust by the Commissioner of Insurance for satisfaction of its liabilities. G.S. Chapter 58, Article 5.

        (2)   Unlike a professional bondsman, there is no statutory limitation on the amount an insurance company may post as bond for a specific defendant.

        (3)   The company's "solvency" for a specific bond, for the purposes of G.S. 15A-537, is determined by the company's POA certificate provided by its bail agent.

            •   The POA certificate offered when executing a bond must be issued by an insurance company for which the agent currently is authorized to execute bonds, as shown on the *Surety Report.*

            •   The dollar amount shown on the POA certificate must, by itself, be sufficient to cover the full amount of the bond. POA certificates may not be "stacked" with other security to satisfy a single Appearance Bond. *See* section IV, below.

        Note that this is different from "splitting," in which multiple, separate bonds are posted to satisfy the monetary condition of a single release order. If local policy allows splitting, a POA <u>might</u> be acceptable to post one of the multiple bonds. See section IV at the end of this outline on stacking versus splitting.

    iii.   **Completing the AOC-CR-201: Bond Secured by Insurance Company**

        (1)   Complete all fields in the form's header.

        (2)   Be sure to include <u>all</u> offenses and file numbers for which the bond will secure the defendant's appearance, *i.e.*, the same cases listed on the Release Order.

        (3)   Check the box for "☐ **Surety Appearance Bond**" and the box immediately below it concerning the "Affidavit" on the reverse side of the form.

        (4)   Complete <u>all</u> fields under **INSURANCE COMPANY**.

            •   Enter the bail agent's <u>personal</u> name on the bond, not the name of any company under which the bail agent conducts business (*e.g.*, "XYZ Bail Bonding"). A bail agent is licensed only in his or her <u>personal</u> capacity, not under a business name.

        (5)   Attach the insurance company's power of attorney (POA) certificate to the bond in the space indicated on side two.

            •   Verify that the POA certificate offered by the bail agent is issued by the same insurance company entered on the bond.

            •   Verify that the POA certificate is for a dollar value of at least the dollar amount of the bond.

        (6)   Have the bail agent complete the **AFFIDAVIT** on side two.

(7) Have both the defendant and the surety sworn or affirmed to the bond, have both sign the bond in the fields for their signatures, and then complete the section titled "**SWORN AND SUBSCRIBED TO BEFORE ME.**"

iv. Motor club bonds.

(1) A motor club bond is a special type of bond governed by the State's insurance statutes. It is posted to ensure the defendant's appearance for certain motor vehicle offenses. G.S. 58-69-2(3)b.

(2) A motor club bond is not secured by the assets of the motor club. It is secured by a domestic or foreign surety (insurance) company authorized to do business in the State. G.S. 58-69-50(a).

- The insurance company securing a motor club bond is not necessarily licensed to conduct bail bond business in the State and therefore might not appear on the *Surety Report*.
- The *Surety Report* does not determine whether or not a motor club bond can be accepted. The bond should be accepted if it otherwise meets the criteria described below.

(3) A motor club bond certificate (frequently appearing on the back of a membership card) is sufficient to secure a bond of up to $1,500, unless the defendant is charged with

- an impaired driving offense or
- any felony.

G.S. 58-69-55.

(4) The judicial official taking a motor club bond should read the bond certificate carefully for other limitations and should refuse the bond if any of its limitations apply to the defendant's case.

- *Amount limitations.* Although G.S. 58-69-50 permits a motor club bond to secure a bond of up to $1,500, the certificate offered might limit the company's liability to a lesser amount.
- *Offense limitations.* Some motor club bonds disclaim liability if posted to secure the defendant's appearance for a long list of offenses in addition to impaired driving and felonies.
- *Expiration dates.* Because they are based on membership, many motor club bond certificates have an expiration date and secure the defendant's appearance only up to that date.

Bonds with expiration dates generally should <u>not</u> be accepted unless the official taking the bond can say with a high degree of certainty that the entire case will be resolved by that date.

(5) **Completing the AOC-CR-201: Bond Secured by Motor Club**

- The NCAOC's NCAWARE application does not recognize motor clubs as licensed sureties.
  - Because motor clubs and their surety companies are not necessarily on the list of insurance companies registered to conduct bail bond business in the State, they are not available for selection as sureties in the Magistrate System or NCAWARE.
  - In order to complete the Appearance Bond electronically, the motor club must be recorded as if the club is an "**ACCOMMODATION BONDSMAN.**"

- The Appearance Bond should be prepared as a "**Surety Appearance Bond**" because the bond is secured by the motor club (or its surety company) as surety, but it is not an insurance company bond. Only the defendant will execute the bond.
  - Complete all fields in the form's header.
  - Be sure to include <u>all</u> offenses and file numbers for which the bond will secure the defendant's appearance, *i.e.,* the same cases listed on the Release Order.
  - Check the box for "☐ **Surety Appearance Bond.**"
  - Record the motor club's information on the bond under **ACCOMMODATION BONDSMAN**. No agent will sign for the club.
  - Attach the motor club bond card or certificate to the court's copy of the Appearance Bond for delivery to the clerk.
  - Have the defendant swear or affirm to the bond and sign the bond in the signature field and then complete the section titled "**SWORN AND SUBSCRIBED TO BEFORE ME.**"
- f. Accommodation Bondsmen.
  - i. Definitions. There are two definitions for accommodation bondsmen in the statute; the relevant elements of both are listed below.
    - (1) Natural person. G.S. 15A-531(1).
      - An accommodation bondsman must be an actual human being.
      - Corporations, partnerships, churches, and other non-human entities <u>cannot</u> be accommodation bondsmen.
    - (2) Who has reached the age of 18. G.S. 15A-531(1).
    - (3) Resident of this State. G.S. 15A-531(1).
    - (4) Receives no compensation. An accommodation bondsman "[s]hall not charge a fee or receive any consideration for action as surety," G.S. 58-71-1(1), and "aside from love and affection and release of the [defendant], receives no consideration for action as surety," G.S. 15A-531(1).
    - (5) Endorses the bail bond. G.S. 15A-531(1); G.S. 58-71-1(1).
    - (6) Provides "satisfactory evidences of ownership, value and marketability of real or personal property to the extent necessary to reasonably satisfy the official taking bond that [such / the] real or personal property will in all respects be sufficient to assure that the full principal sum of the bond will be realized [in the event of / if there is a] breach of the conditions [thereof / of the bond]." [G.S. 15A-531(1) / G.S. 58-71-1(1)]
  - ii. Who cannot be an accommodation bondsman?
    - (1) Judicial and criminal justice officials and employees are prohibited from serving as a surety for anyone other than certain family members.
    - (2) G.S. 15A-541 prohibits any of the following persons from serving as surety for anyone other than their "immediate family": "sheriff, deputy sheriff, other law-enforcement officer, judicial official, attorney, parole officer, probation officer, jailer, assistant jailer, employee of the General Court of Justice, other public employee assigned to duties relating to the administration of criminal justice, *or spouse of any such person.*"
      - The statue further prohibits any such person from becoming an agent of a bonding company or a professional bondsman and

from having any financial interest, direct or indirect, in the affairs of any firm or corporation "whose principal business is acting as a bondsman."

- Violation is a Class 2 misdemeanor.
- "Immediate family" is not defined in Chapter 15A but may be broader than the traditional understanding of parents, spouse, children, and siblings due to the relationships named in the companion provision, G.S. 58-71-105.

(3) G.S. 58-71-105 prohibits conduct substantively identical to that prohibited in G.S. 15A-541.

- The prohibition applies to posting bond for any person except the prospective surety's "spouse, parent, brother, sister, child, or descendant."
- "Descendant" is not normally within the scope of "immediate family," so G.S. 58-71-105 may allow criminal justice officials more latitude in posting bonds for family (*e.g.*, grandchildren) than the language of G.S. 15A-541 would suggest.
- Violation is a Class 1 misdemeanor. G.S. 58-71-185.

iii. No blank bonds. Like a professional bondsman or bail agent, an accommodation bondsman may not sign bonds "in blank" for another person to execute on the accommodation bondsman's behalf. G.S. 58-71-110. Violation of this prohibition is a Class 1 misdemeanor. G.S. 58-71-185.

iv. "Solvency" of accommodation bondsmen.

(1) The standard for finding an accommodation bondsman "sufficiently solvent" for the bond, as required by G.S. 15A-537, is found in both definitions of accommodation bondsmen:

> "satisfactory evidences of ownership, value and marketability of real or personal property . . . sufficient to assure that the full principal sum of the bond will be realized" in the event of a breach.

G.S. 15A-531(1); G.S. 58-71-1(1).

(2) The official taking the bond can be satisfied as to the surety's solvency on the basis of personal property, alone.

(3) The "evidences of ownership, value and marketability" of property may be established by any source that the official taking the bond deems reliable. The local bond policy may specify evidence that the judicial official should consider.

(4) Common sources for determining the value of real property or the owner's equity therein, with their relative merits and shortcomings, include

- *Tax office records*. These may give accurate value but will miss such encumbrances as outstanding judgments, liens, or senior mortgages and deeds of trust.
- *Register of deeds*. The Register's records will include encumbrances on the prospective surety's real property, such as mortgages or deeds of trust, but they will omit judgments and other liens and do not provide an accurate account of the surety's equity in the property.

- *Judgments Index.* The index of civil judgments maintained by the clerk of superior court will identify judgments and liens against the prospective surety's real property, but it provides no evidence of the property's value or the surety's ability to convey good title.
- *Title opinion.* A full title opinion by an attorney is the most comprehensive way to determine equity and marketability, but it is the most burdensome (and expensive) for the surety.

(5) The surety's equity in property offered to demonstrate solvency must be sufficient to cover the amount of the bond over and above the constitutional exemptions that the surety could claim at enforcement of any judgment thereon.

- For real property, the homestead exemption is $1,000. The personal property exemption is $500. N.C. Const. art. X, §§ 1–2.
- The official taking the bond does not need to consider statutory exemptions, because they do not apply to a forfeiture judgment. G.S. 1C-1601(e)(2).

(6) Most local bond policies permit an accommodation bondsman who has demonstrated sufficient solvency to execute a bond below a certain dollar amount solely on the surety's signature (*i.e.*, without posting specific security, such as cash or a deed of trust, to real property).

Completing AOC-CR-201: Bond Secured by Accommodation Bondsman (Without Specific Security)

- Complete all fields in the form's header.
- Be sure to include <u>all</u> offenses and file numbers for which the bond will secure the defendant's appearance, *i.e.*, the same cases listed on the Release Order.
- Check the box for "□ **Surety Appearance Bond.**"
- Complete all fields under **ACCOMMODATION BONDSMAN** with the surety's information.
- Have both the defendant and the surety(ies) sworn or affirmed to the bond, have both sign the bond in the fields for their signatures, and complete the section titled "**SWORN AND SUBSCRIBED TO BEFORE ME.**"

(7) False qualification by surety. It is a Class 2 misdemeanor for a prospective surety to "sign an appearance bond . . . knowing or having reason to know that he does not own sufficient property over and above his exemption allowed by law to enable him to pay the bond should it be ordered forfeited." G.S. 15A-542.

(8) Specific collateral/security for an accommodation bondsman.

- Unlike a bond secured by a mortgage on the defendant's property under G.S. 15A-534(a)(4) and G.S. 58-74-5, there is no statute specifically authorizing an enforceable security interest in real property of a surety. However, local bond policies typically specify a threshold dollar amount of a bond for which specific security (*i.e.*, a deed of trust to real property) will be required.
- Cash in the full amount of the bond is always acceptable.

- The ultimate beneficiary of any forfeiture of the bond, the local schools, undoubtedly will prefer cash in lieu of a property bond because enforcement of the forfeiture judgment requires no additional court action (*i.e.*, no foreclosure proceeding).
- See section III.B of this outline, above, for guidance when accepting cash as a surety's security for the bond, particularly "Cash Deposited by a Third Party" and "Cash Bonds Greater Than $10,000."

- Property Bonds
  - Terminology. It is important to be clear what is meant by a "property bond."
    - Some officials use the term to mean any bond posted by an accommodation bondsman (other than cash), regardless of whether or not an actual deed of trust is recorded against a specific parcel of real property to secure that bond. In this scenario, the bond is secured merely by the surety's promise that he or she is able to cover the bond, as demonstrated by his or her ownership of property, generally. The fact that a surety proved the ownership and value of a specific parcel of realty as evidence of his or her solvency does <u>not</u> give the State an enforceable or priority interest in that parcel. Other liens or encumbrances might intervene after the posting of the bond that would prevent the State from collecting against that parcel (*i.e.*, via the Sheriff's levy under a writ of execution), but the surety's other property—real and personal—remains subject to levy in the event of execution on a judgment of forfeiture for that bond.
    - Another use of the term "property bond" means that the surety has recorded a deed of trust to a specific parcel (or parcels) with the Register of Deeds in the county (or counties) where the land lies, naming the clerk of superior court as trustee on the deed and conditioning its power of sale on satisfaction of the bond obligation in a specific case. In this scenario, the State has an enforceable interest in that specific parcel, which can be sold at foreclosure to satisfy a judgment of forfeiture and which has priority over subsequent liens or encumbrances against the surety's assets.
    - This outline uses "property bond" in the latter sense: a bond secured by a deed of trust properly recorded and securing the surety's obligation under a specific Appearance Bond.
  - The considerations below for accepting a property bond from a surety apply also to deeds of trust posted by the defendant to his own property (in lieu of a mortgage). The only difference is that the Appearance Bond secured by the defendant's own

property is executed by the defendant, only, while a property bond by a surety requires that the surety execute the bond as an accommodation bondsman.

- The deed of trust must be executed by <u>all</u> owners of an enforceable interest in the property, and <u>all</u> of those parties must sign the Appearance Bond as sureties.
  - Each surety on a property bond must meet the qualifications of an accommodation bondsman. No property owned in whole or in part by a minor, by a non-resident, or by any non-human entity may be used to post a property bond.
  - No promissory note is required. The Appearance Bond is the evidence of the debt secured by the deed. However, many local bond policies still require a separate promissory note.
  - The deed of trust (or the promissory note, if required locally) must identify the Appearance Bond secured by the deed.
- Judicial officials should be cautious about accepting a deed of trust to rented property.
  - Federal law enacted in 2009 provides that buyers at foreclosure must honor most existing leases of the foreclosed property. Helping Families Save Their Homes Act of 2009, Pub. L. No. 111-22.
  - Because a buyer at foreclosure must honor existing leases on the property, a judicial official asked to accept a bond secured by a deed of trust to property under lease should consider the effect that the lease might have on the property's "marketability"—one of the factors a judicial official must consider when evaluating property as proof of an accommodation bondsman's solvency. G.S. 15A-531(1).
  - The federal legislation in question originally was due to expire on December 31, 2012, but it was extended until December 31, 2014, by Pub. L. No. 111-203 (the Dodd-Frank Wall Street Reform and Consumer Protection Act). A judicial official presented with a deed of trust to leased property after December 2014 should verify whether or not the federal law has been extended again before considering the lease an impairment of the property's marketability.
- The deed of trust must identify the three parties to the deed:
  - Grantor(s): Owner(s) of the property, who must execute the bond as surety(ies).
  - Beneficiary: "State of North Carolina, f/b/o [Charging] County Board of Education"
  - Trustee: "[Charging] County Clerk of Superior Court." The clerk should not be referred to by name because

the clerk is the trustee in his or her official, not personal, capacity.

Note: If the drafter insists on including the clerk's personal name, the full trustee designation should include the clerk's "successors in office." *E.g.*, "Jane Doe, Clerk of Superior Court of Black County or her successor in office," which makes it clear that the trustee is the office, not Jane Doe in her personal capacity.

○ **Completing the AOC-CR-201: Bond Secured by Accommodation Bondsman (Property Bond)**

Note: If the deed of trust is executed by the defendant to his or her own property, prepare the Appearance Bond as described for a mortgage bond in section III.C, above.

 – Complete all fields in the form's header.

 – Be sure to include <u>all</u> offenses and file numbers for which the bond will secure the defendant's appearance, *i.e.*, the same cases listed on the Release Order.

 – Check the box for "☐ **Surety Appearance Bond.**"

 – Complete all fields under **ACCOMMODATION BONDSMAN** with the surety's information.

 Note: If more than two property owners will serve as surety, enter the information for the third and any subsequent sureties on form AOC-CR-201A and include it with the Appearance Bond.

 – Have both the defendant and surety(ies) sworn or affirmed to the bond, have both sign the bond in the fields for their signatures, and complete the section titled "**SWORN AND SUBSCRIBED TO BEFORE ME.**"

 – The court's copy of the deed of trust must be included with the court's copy of the Appearance Bond for delivery to the clerk.

• Common questions about property bonds.

 ○ Case in County A, Property in County B.

  – Because local bond policies are set by local officials for cases pending within that jurisdiction, the bond policy of the county where the charge is pending should be followed whenever possible.

  – The deed of trust must be registered in the county where the property lies, but the court's copy of the deed should be delivered along with the Appearance Bond to the clerk of the charging county, and the clerk of the <u>charging</u> county must be the trustee on the deed.

  – The official taking the bond makes an independent judgment about the surety's solvency and should not ask other court officials to "certify," "verify," or otherwise provide an opinion about the surety's solvency or the value or equity of specific property. *See* Joan G. Brannon & Ann M. Anderson, North Carolina Clerk of Superior Court

PROCEDURES MANUAL, 22.9 (UNC School of Government, 2012).
- ◦ Property owned by defendant and spouse.
  - – Because a defendant, by definition, is not a "surety," some jurisdictions prohibit securing a bond with property jointly owned by a defendant and another person (*e.g.*, a spouse).
  - – If, however, the Appearance Bond is executed by all owners of an enforceable interest in the property—with the defendant executing the bond as defendant and the spouse executing in the capacity of a surety—any judgment of forfeiture on the bond should be enforceable by execution. It is an unsettled question whether or not the deed of trust subsequently would be foreclosable in the event the judgment is not satisfied by execution.
  - – Note that this is different from the rule that an actual mortgage posted by the defendant for a bond must be to property owned solely by the defendant. *See* section III.C.4 of this appendix, above.

IV. Stacking and Splitting Bonds

A. There is no statutory definition or guidance for the common practices of stacking and splitting bonds; the typical scenarios in which the terms are used are described below.

B. Because there is no guidance in statute or in appellate case law, judicial officials should adhere to any local bond policies for either practice in lieu of any contrary guidance below.

C. Stacking: Executing a <u>single</u> Appearance Bond to satisfy the monetary condition of a release order using multiple ("stacked") forms of security, none of which individually covers the full amount of the bond.

> *Example:* A bail agent and the defendant's girlfriend execute a single Appearance Bond to satisfy a $100,000 condition of release, attaching to the bond a POA certificate from the agent's insurance company worth $60,000 and a deed of trust to girlfriend's property for $40,000.

1. By signing the same bond for $100,000, the sureties are jointly and severally liable for the <u>entire</u> $100,000, but <u>neither</u> has demonstrated solvency for that amount. Because neither has met the solvency standard of G.S. 15A-537, <u>stacking never should be allowed</u>.

2. Insurance companies present an additional problem when stacking. In addition to failure to demonstrate solvency for the entire amount, the POA certificates may be void when stacked.
   a. Almost all POA certificates disclaim any liability of the insurance company if the certificate is used in conjunction with another POA certificate (whether from the same or another insurance company) to post a single defendant's bond.
   b. In addition, some companies' POA certificates disclaim liability if joined with any other security (*e.g.*, the girlfriend's deed of trust) for the same bond or the same defendant.

3. Note that it is not stacking when multiple accommodation bondsmen post a single piece of jointly owned security (such as the defendant's parents posting a deed of trust to a single parcel of property). Stacking refers only to the combination of multiple forms of security to post a bond, not the presence of multiple sureties.

D. Splitting: Executing <u>multiple</u> Appearance Bonds to satisfy a monetary condition of release, with each bond secured by a different surety or different form of security.

> *Example:* A bail agent and the defendant's girlfriend execute separate Appearance Bonds to satisfy a $100,000 condition of release: the first Appearance Bond for $60,000, secured by a POA certificate from the insurance company, and a second Appearance Bond for $40,000, secured by a deed of trust to the girlfriend's property.

1. Whether or not to allow a splitting sometimes is addressed by local bond policies.
2. Some officials disallow splitting for the same concerns about solvency as with stacking. Because neither surety has demonstrated solvency for the full monetary condition of release, it is possible that neither meets the "sufficiently solvent" standard of G.S. 15A-537. Other officials permit splitting because each surety has demonstrated solvency for his or her limited portion of the total.
3. If local practice permits splitting, each surety must sign a <u>separate</u> Appearance Bond for his or her specific portion of the total. The defendant must sign <u>all</u> of the split Appearance Bonds.
4. A judicial official taking bonds should be wary of splitting that is really stacking in disguise.
   (1) In particular, any POA certificate offered by a bail agent to satisfy part of a split bond should be reviewed carefully to ensure that its disclaimers of liability do not prohibit its use in conjunction with other security to post a bond for a single defendant or for the same case.
   (2) *Example:* A bail agent wants to sign two bonds to meet the total monetary condition of release, using two POA certificates from the same company to attach to the two bonds. Because of the disclaimers of liability in the POA certificates, neither is adequate to secure the bond obligation.

V. Taking Bonds for Defendants with Immigration Detainers

A. A defendant sometimes is confined in a North Carolina jail on a Release Order (AOC-CR-200) for a pending North Carolina case and also on a "detainer" issued by Immigration and Customs Enforcement (ICE) of the U.S. Department of Homeland Security.

B. Article 26 (Bail) of Chapter 15A of the General Statutes does not account for federal immigration actions when determining whether or not to allow a defendant or surety to execute a bond.
   1. The procedures for taking a bond to satisfy the State release order are independent of the federal action.
   2. A judicial official presented with a bond for the defendant's State proceeding should proceed as if the detainer did not exist; the defendant or surety may execute a bond as normal.
   3. Although the detainer has no direct effect on whether or not to take the bond for the State proceeding, the judicial official taking the bond may wish to inform the defendant and any surety that the detainer exists and that posting bond will not secure the defendant's immediate release. However, satisfying the State conditions of release is a necessary

precedent to begin ICE's 48-hour window in which to take custody of the defendant, as described below.

C. A detainer is a directive issued by ICE to the law enforcement agency having custody of the defendant. 8 C.F.R. § 287.7. When taking a bond for a defendant with a detainer, the judicial official taking the bond should be aware that the detainer accomplishes two things:

1. it requests that the law enforcement agency inform ICE when the person is about to be released from custody, 8 C.F.R. § 287.7(a), and

2. it directs the law enforcement agency to hold a person "not otherwise detained" by the agency for up to 48 hours (excluding Saturdays, Sundays, and holidays) to permit ICE to take custody of the person. 8 C.F.R. § 287.7(d).

As long as the conditions of release for the pending State proceeding have not been met, the defendant is "otherwise detained," so ICE's 48-hour deadline does not begin to run.

D. Requests for "Refunds" of Bonds Posted for ICE Detainees.

1. An ICE detainer does not relieve a surety of the obligation to ensure the defendant's appearance in a State proceeding (though defendant's detention by ICE at the time of a future failure to appear might constitute grounds for setting aside any forfeiture of the bond, pursuant to G.S. 15A-544.5(b)(7)). Therefore the defendant or surety is not entitled to a refund or cancellation of the bond based solely on the existence of an ICE detainer.

2. If a surety, upon learning of the detainer, wishes to be relieved of the bond obligation, he or she must meet one of the conditions of G.S. 15A-534(h). Because the defendant's case likely has not reached final disposition when the surety learns of the detainer, as a practical matter this requires either

   • a judge's order releasing the surety from the obligation, G.S. 15A-534(h)(1), or
   • surrender of the defendant, G.S. 15A-534(h)(2).

3. If the surety is released from the obligation or carries out an effective surrender, the bond should not be destroyed or given to the former surety.

   a. Once executed, a bond and all associated material must be delivered to the clerk's office for filing. G.S. 15A-537(b).

   b. All records associated with the bond, including professional bondsmen's seals (the gold stickers) and insurance company power of attorney (POA) certificates, are part of the court's record and therefore may not be destroyed or removed from the court's custody. A surety may <u>not</u> get the bondsman's seal or POA certificate back once the bond has been executed.

   c. Any refund of any cash bond after a judge's order has released the surety or after a valid surrender will be processed by the clerk's office and sent via check to the person identified as the owner on the Appearance Bond.